Eat, Memory

ALSO BY AMANDA HESSER

The Cook and the Gardener

Cooking for Mr. Latte

W. W. Norton & Company

New York London

Eat, Memory

Great Writers at the Table

A COLLECTION OF ESSAYS FROM

THE *NEW YORK TIMES*

Edited by Amanda Hesser

Manufacturing by The Haddon Craftsmen, Inc.
Book design by Chris Welch

Library of Congress Cataloging-in-Publication Data

Eat, memory : great writers at the table : a collection of essays from the New York Times
/ edited by Amanda Hesser.—1st ed.
p. cm.
ISBN 978-0-393-06763-7 (hardcover)
1. Food. 2. Cookery. I. Hesser, Amanda.
TX355.5.E25 2008
641.5—dc22   2008036125

W. W. Norton & Company, Inc., 500 Fifth Avenue, New York, N.Y. 10110
www.wwnorton.com

W. W. Norton & Company Ltd., Castle House, 75/76 Wells Street London W1T 3QT

1 2 3 4 5 6 7 8 9 0

CONTENTS

CONTENTS

STRUGGLES

LOSS

INTRODUCTION

Writers know that if you want to portray a person succinctly, tellingly, you describe the way he eats. Food is the royal road to the unconscious.

In *Love Medicine*, Louise Erdrich introduces Lulu by how she butters bread:

> "My my my," he said to Lulu now. She was buttering a piece of bread soft as the plump undersides of her arms. "Lot of water under the dam."

She agreed, taking alert nips of her perfectly covered slice. She had sprinkled a teaspoon of sugar over it, carefully distributing the grains. That was how she was.

Lulu's precision with the sugar and her wolfish "nips" at the bread tell us who she is: someone controlled and territorial.

In both fiction and nonfiction, the sound of fat snapping in a pan sets the mood of a place; the hurried peeling of carrots or a sink of abandoned dishes suggest the pressures of everyday life. Food is also, sometimes unfortunately, one of the favorite subjects of simile—(he had fists like hams, a nose like a wet potato). And this is all because we spend most of our time at home in and around the kitchen—because food is the most familiar and universal medium in our lives.

When I think back to when my father moved out of the house for a few months when I was eight, my recollection is always accompanied by a taste —that of the filet mignon at the French restaurant he took me to on one of my visits to his makeshift lodgings. When I think of his long last illness, I remember making toast in my parents' kitchen—something easy and elemental. And the births of my twin son and daughter are inseparable in memory from what sustained me in the hospital: sweet plums and peppermint tea. Each of these ordinary tastes, when amplified by powerful feelings, becomes a sensual beacon that illuminates a whole swath of my life. The food doesn't matter, really. What it evokes does.

In my view, not enough gets written about this emotional component of the way we eat. When I became the food editor of the *New York Times Magazine* in 2004, I attempted to change this with a new column called "Eat, Memory." I asked well-known writers—playwrights, screenwriters, novelists, poets, journalists—to contribute essays about an important moment in their lives that involved food. Many of the resulting stories are collected in this book.

There was just one rule: nothing sentimental. No one wants to read an overwrought paean to grandma's corn bread. But we might well be interested in why your grandma made it whenever she was lonely.

As un-rosy but riveting stories began to pour in, I realized that many food memories capture times of difficulty and sadness; these less happy passages are often the ones that change and define us. Chang-rae Lee recalled his futile attempts to nourish his very ill mother and how he made carefully composed meals to stave off accepting her death. John Burnham Schwartz had a friend whose passion for cooking was so maniacal that soon he had no one left around him to cook for. Pico Iyer discovered that even in a global culture, you can become emotionally connected to a neighborhood chain store—as he did with his local Lawson in Japan—and be devastated when it closes. And the novelist Ann Patchett reexamined her stubbornness in a heated argument she once had with her then boyfriend, now husband, over dinner at the famed Paris restaurant Taillevent. Their relationship almost dissolved before the petits-fours.

Of course, the passions aroused by foods and meals aren't always gloomy. Colson Whitehead worked himself into a happy lather over his hatred of ice cream. Dawn Drzal found that having lunch with M.F.K. Fisher, the grand dame of literary food writing, was a mix of stress and sly wit and a most unusual parting gift. And Allen Shawn, an English professor at Bennington, wrote of his autistic twin sister Mary, who lives in an institution and seems shut out from many of life's pleasures. Throughout her life, Shawn's family planned an annual lunch with Mary, and always made sure the menu was precisely the same, out of fear that any irregularity would unsettle her and spoil their time together. Shawn wrote of the year the menu did change, and what happened.

Americans' guilt-ridden relationship with food provoked both satire and self-deprecation. George Saunders wrote about going on an all-air, no-food diet that caused him to gain seventy pounds. Patricia Marx argued that precisely because she never eats, she's the consummate hostess. And Tom Perrotta explained how his long list of food aversions almost landed him in an East German prison.

For chefs, who couple artistry with blue-collar labor, every day is a patchwork of small battles. Dan Barber, the chef and an owner of Blue Hill in Greenwich Village, explored the pressures to innovate, to provide diners and even his staff with the promise of new flavors, and the trick he once resorted to when he couldn't deliver the goods. When Gabrielle Hamilton hired a blind cook at her East Village restaurant Prune, he led her into ethical terrain she wasn't prepared to navigate.

Like ambitious recipes tried for the first time, these stories often don't turn out quite as expected. But the results—to my taste, at least—are all the more glorious for the surprises these writers allow us to see and savor. Bon appétit.

Illusions

Paris Match

ANN PATCHETT

Ann Patchett's books include Bel Canto, Truth & Beauty, Run *and* What Now?

There are things people do when they are first in love: they surprise each other with trips to Paris; they make reservations at impossibly expensive restaurants; they have conversations about former lovers while they eat. All of these things can happen after years of marriage as well, but the chances are infinitely smaller.

Karl and I had been together a little more than a year. He arranged the trip, and I made the reservations for a very late lunch. I can't remember how it all got started, but as we sat in Taillevent, at such a beautiful table right in the center of the room, the conversation somehow turned to Mark. My relationship with Mark had been an amicable one that had come to a mostly amicable end. Karl asked if we fought a lot. Or maybe I asked Karl if he fought with his ex-wife, and so in return he asked me about Mark.

The waiter came and handed me a wine list the size of a tombstone. I turned the pages for a moment, the way I might have turned the pages of a calculus exam, with some interest and not a single spark of comprehension. "White," I said, and Karl, who doesn't drink, just shook his head.

"The worst fight we ever had wasn't exactly a fight," I said. "We were playing a word game. When he told me about it, I said I wanted to play, but then I couldn't figure out the answer, and he wouldn't stop. He just kept playing it and playing it and, I don't know—"

The waiter came to take our orders. We ordered something. Some food.

"What?" Karl asked after the waiter had gone.

I remembered the fight very clearly. We were in the car, and Mark was driving, and when we got to a red light I opened the door and got out. I walked through the traffic to the curb, something I have never done before or since. "I thought I was going to kill him."

"So what's the game?" he asked.

"It isn't hard. That's what's so awful about it. Once I actually got it, it was simple."

Karl sat back. He was beautiful in the rich light, beautiful between the damask draperies and the thick white tablecloth. He rested his fingers against the heavy fork beside his plate. "Tell me how to play. I'm good at these sorts of things."

We hadn't been together long enough to know that we shouldn't talk about old lovers. We probably hadn't been together long enough to go to Paris. No two people are ever together long enough to enjoy word games.

The waiter returned and poured the wine into my glass right from the bottle, which struck me as very sophisticated. Our appetizers came. They were something I wanted. Something I had chosen carefully. I remember that when I bit into whatever it was, I closed my eyes, stunned that anything could be so delicate, so delicious. "I say a word, and then I tell you if the word is or isn't it. For example"—I picked up my wineglass—"it is glass, but it isn't wine."

Karl nodded.

"Now you can ask me one word, and I'll tell you if it is or it isn't, and we keep going until you figure out what the difference is."

"Is it a plate?" he asked.

"It isn't a plate, but it is a bottle."

He waited a minute. He thought it over. "I don't get it."

"It takes some time," I said. "It's a rabbit, but it's not a box."

He finished his appetizer, whatever it was. He didn't offer me a bite. "I don't know."

"It's a tree, but it isn't a leaf."

"I give up," he said.

"It's Woody, but it isn't Mia."

"I don't know," he said. "Tell me."

I went on for a while, not telling him, throwing out words in patterns that irritated him profoundly. The main course arrived. I can very nearly smell it now. It was so succulent, complex, divine, but I cannot for the life of me say what it was. "It's pretty," I said, "but it isn't shoes."

"Stop it."

"It isn't stop or go or wait." Even as I said it, I could see myself stepping out of the car into traffic. It is traffic. I had told Mark I was through if he didn't tell me the answer. I said it much more colorfully than that. But when the answer came to me later, an easy lightning bolt slicing open my head, I wasn't angry anymore. I got it. It had taken me more than an hour, but I got it, and that joy, so sudden and unexpected, was the reward.

The waiter kept refilling my glass, though I don't remember asking him to. The desserts were sublime, and we pushed them aside. The bill—I do remember that much—was $350. We may as well have piled the money on the table and put a match to it. It was the best meal either one of us had ever had in our lives, and we missed it.

"I'm glad I found out now what kind of person you are," Karl said. He had never been so angry at me, not before or since. I knew how he felt. As we were walking away from the restaurant, I broke down and told him. I did it because he was walking so quickly and my heels were too high and I didn't know how to get back to the hotel alone. I told him, and I ruined everything. Mark had been smarter to weather my fury so that I could find the answer for myself, because once I found it, I forgave him. Karl, on the other hand, just stayed mad. He told me I was cruel and cold, and the next night at L'Arpège he told me it was over.

"You're not breaking up with me in a fish restaurant in Paris," I said. "Not over this."

And so he didn't. We stayed together for ten years after that, and then we married. It has been a very happy union. Our fight at Taillevent is a tattoo on our relationship, though. Neither of us will ever forget it, but it all strikes me as funny now. The sad part is that the meal is gone forever. It's a fault of our brains to remember the fight while forgetting the sole. Was it sole? I know what I said, but I can only dream about what I must have eaten.

·

TAILLEVENT'S CREAM OF WATERCRESS SOUP
WITH CAVIAR

FOR THE SOUP BASE

3 tablespoons unsalted butter

1 pound leeks (about 2 large), white and light green parts only, halved, rinsed and thinly sliced

1 onion, finely chopped
Pinch fine sea salt
1 quart chicken stock, preferably homemade
2 cups heavy cream or whole milk

3 tablespoons coarse sea salt
1 pound watercress (about 3 bunches), stems removed, leaves
   rinsed
1 cup heavy cream
Juice of 1 lemon
Fine sea salt and freshly ground white pepper
2 tablespoons osetra or other caviar

1. To make the soup base: Melt the butter in a 6-quart stockpot
   over medium heat. Stir in the leeks, onion and salt. Cover and
   cook over low heat until the vegetables are soft but not browned,
   about 3 minutes. Add the chicken stock and cream. Raise the
   heat to medium-high and bring to a gentle boil, then simmer
   on low, uncovered, for 30 minutes.

2. Purée the soup in a blender or food processor until emulsified
   and smooth. Return the mixture to the stockpot and set over
   medium-high heat. Bring to a gentle boil. Using a slotted spoon,
   skim off any impurities that rise to the surface. Set aside or cover
   and refrigerate for up to 24 hours.

3. To finish the soup: Fill a large bowl with ice water and set aside. Bring 4 quarts water to a boil. Add the coarse sea salt and watercress. Blanch until wilted and soft, 2 to 3 minutes. Immediately drain the watercress, then plunge into the ice water to stop the cooking. Drain again; do not squeeze out all the water. Purée the watercress in a food processor, then place it in a fine-meshed sieve and press out any remaining liquid. Discard the liquid. Set the purée aside.

4. When ready to serve, reheat the soup base over low heat. Meanwhile, using an electric mixer, whip the cream to stiff peaks. Stir in the lemon juice and season to taste with sea salt and white pepper. Just before serving, add the watercress purée to the warmed soup and stir until blended. Ladle the soup into shallow soup bowls. Place a scoop of whipped cream in the center of each bowl and top with a small spoonful of caviar.

Serves 6

Adapted from *The Paris Cookbook* by Patricia Wells.

The Great Carrot Caper

DAN BARBER

*Dan Barber is the executive chef and co-owner of Blue Hill and
Blue Hill at Stone Barns.*

L ast December, right around Christmas, I received a small
package from Jean-Marc Montegottero, an artisanal nut
oil producer in Burgundy. The package contained a
shoebox filled with dust. Flummoxed, I phoned his American dis-
tributor and importer and our mutual friend, Olivier Wittmann,
to inquire about this strange gift.

The dust was almond residue, Olivier said, and he told me about
a visit he'd made to Jean-Marc's on a cold October afternoon. As
he walked up the path to his farmhouse, all he could smell was
almonds. Figuring that Jean-Marc was making an almond tart for

dessert, he opened the door to the kitchen and saw only a large sautoir of potatoes simmering gently in duck fat. Confused, he looked at Jean-Marc, who simply smiled. "Sit," he said. "Eat."

The potatoes smelled, and tasted, as Olivier would attest, like almond potatoes. Jean-Marc, a scrupulous recycler, collected the flourlike dust after pressing almonds for the oil and spread it over his potato field like compost. Through a kind of magical osmosis, the almond potatoes were born.

And why not? Burgundy's clay soil is famous for imparting earthy tones to its wine, and "pre-sale" lamb gets nourished by the salty marsh grass of the bay of Mont Saint-Michel, so why couldn't almonds infuse their flavor into potatoes?

Jean-Marc's gift to me could not have come at a better time. Fall harvest at Stone Barns was a waning memory. Dark clouds of root vegetables and cabbages were on the horizon. I seized on the nut idea—with carrots instead of potatoes. Almonds and carrots are a better pairing, I thought. (Was this becoming competitive?)

Getting the cooks excited about the connections to the farm became one goal of the project. (Carlo Petrini, the founder of Slow Food, has often said that we ought not to think of ourselves as consumers but more as coproducers who are connected to the food we eat. Here was our chance.) But even more, I wanted them to know that their chef was always pushing for creativity and experimentation. Ferran Adrià may have espresso foam and olive oil capsules, I thought, but he doesn't have carrots pre-infused with almonds. At night I dreamed of being on the cover of *Gourmet* magazine wearing a black cowboy hat and cradling a bundle of carrots. Headline: "Chefs as Farmers-Scientists: The New Frontier in Food."

In the days that followed, the farmers dutifully (and skeptically) planted Napoli carrots and spread the almond dust over the rows. Meanwhile, I told the staff—first the cooks, then the waiters, then anyone who would listen—that we were engaged in a very exciting experiment. "A revolutionary harvest," I called it. But I said nothing about Jean-Marc. The excitement of being a creator–farmer–mad scientist was too intoxicating; I couldn't admit to the truth that I was more of a lucky chef–gentleman farmer–copycat.

I used the next nine weeks as a buildup to the harvest, taking the cooks and waiters down to the greenhouse and showing them the almond carrots. I explained that my plan was to do nothing with them in the kitchen, or almost nothing, just serve them shaved and perhaps with a splash of vinaigrette. This dish would be about the wonders of nature, not about the creativity of the chef (false modesty, of course: in proposing to do nothing to the carrots I hoped everyone would concentrate on the creativity of the idea).

The week before the harvest I intensified the campaign. I spoke about the carrots at every family meal and made sure the cooks went to the greenhouse to weed and care for what was about to make history. I even got the valets excited, proudly showing off our little Manhattan Project. "Jesus, it sort of already smells like almonds," I heard one of the valets say as he walked away. "Goddamn genius," the other said.

The Friday night of the harvest we were overbooked. News of

the almond carrots buzzed in the dining room. For some reason the vegetables arrived a bit late that day, and there was the usual mayhem in prepping for dinner. So I didn't actually try the carrots until service began. How did they taste? Sweet and crisp, very delicious. But not like almonds. Not even a faint whisper of nuttiness. And nothing that suggested nutfulness in the future.

Holding the carrot in my hand, I recognized my creation for what it was—a wish wrapped in a conceit, a chef's folly. And then the orders began trickling in: "Ordering, Table 41, a fennel soup and three almond carrot salads." And then, "Ordering, Table 31, four almond carrot salads followed by . . ." It had begun.

Stunned, I reached for a mandoline and a bowl. I shaved the carrots very thinly, tossing them with lemon vinaigrette, salt, pepper and . . . and I added a splash of Jean-Marc's almond oil.

"Taste these," I said, and handed them around to the cooks and waiters.

"Wow," said Karen, our resident waiter-scholar. "Unbelievable almond flavor."

"They taste like a bowl of almonds," said Duncan, the wide-eyed vegetable cook.

We sold sixty-six almond carrot salads, exhausting the entire day's harvest to great fanfare. I spent the beginning of the night making the salads in a fearful state of self-loathing: Would I be discovered for a fraud, like some South Korean scientist, pulled in front of my deceived coworkers and accused of duplicitous claims?

But there were only compliments and applause, questions about how to get involved with the farm and comment cards in a bulk we had never seen, four big stars written across the bottom of many. It was a hugely energetic night, filled with the wonder of this gentle genetic modification that the entire dining room believed it was experiencing.

Mysteriously, my furtive, last-minute maneuvers can't account for the overwhelming response, and I should know: in the chaos of trying to make so many salads, I often forgot—or was guilt at work here?—to add the almond oil.

"Oh, that doesn't matter," said an amused Karen when I confessed to her—a mini culpa after midnight. "The myth outdid the truth, and you got your almond carrots."

Not long afterward, I received a call from a well-known New York chef I hadn't heard from in years. He called to "catch up," and five minutes into the conversation he said, "Hey, so I heard you're growing some funky nut carrot up there." There was a long pause. "Any for sale?"

ALMOND CARROT SALAD

FOR THE ALMONDS

3/4 cup whole blanched almonds

2 teaspoons sugar

1 teaspoon ground cumin

1 teaspoon olive oil

Juice of half a lemon

Salt and freshly ground white pepper

FOR THE SALAD

1/2 cup golden raisins

1/4 cup white verjus

1 pound carrots, peeled

2 tablespoons white balsamic vinegar

2 teaspoons lemon juice

1 tablespoon almond oil

1 tablespoon extra-virgin olive oil

2 teaspoons minced shallots

Salt and freshly ground white pepper

*1 packed cup mixed whole herbs, including parsley, chervil, dill
    and mint*

1. Prepare the almonds: Preheat the oven to 375 degrees. In a small
   bowl, toss together the almonds, sugar, cumin, olive oil, lemon
   juice and a pinch each of salt and pepper. Spread the almonds
   on a baking sheet and toast until light brown, 10 to 12 minutes.
   Let cool.
2. Make the salad: In a small saucepan, bring the raisins and verjus
   to a boil. Remove from the heat and let cool. Strain the raisins,
   discarding the verjus.

3. Using a mandoline or sharp vegetable peeler, slice the carrots lengthwise into ribbons, applying pressure on the peeler so the ribbons aren't too thin. Place the carrots, vinegar, lemon juice, oils, shallots, cooled almonds and raisins in a large bowl. Season with salt and pepper, mix to combine and marinate for 10 minutes. Gently toss in the herbs and serve.

Serves 4

The Fish

BILLY COLLINS

Billy Collins's latest collection of poems is Ballistics.

As soon as the elderly waiter
placed before me the fish I had ordered,
it began to stare up at me
with its one flat, iridescent eye.

I feel sorry for you, it seemed to say,
eating alone in this awful restaurant
bathed in such unkindly light
and surrounded by these dreadful murals of Sicily.

And I feel sorry for you, too—
yanked from the sea and now lying dead
next to some boiled potatoes in Pittsburgh—
I said back to the fish as I raised my fork.

And thus my dinner in an unfamiliar city
with its rivers and lighted bridges
was graced not only with chilled wine
and lemon slices but with compassion and sorrow

even after the waiter removed my plate
with the head of the fish still staring
and the barrel vault of its delicate bones
terribly exposed, save for a shroud of parsley.

SOLE MEUNIÈRE

1/2 cup flour
2 tablespoons canola oil
2 fillets sole
Salt and freshly ground black pepper
4 tablespoons unsalted butter, diced
2 tablespoons white wine

Juice of 1/2 lemon

1 tablespoon finely chopped flat-leaf parsley

1. Place the flour in a wide dish. In a large nonstick skillet, heat the oil over high. When hot, season the fish generously on both sides with salt and pepper. Cover in flour and then shake off excess. Cook in the oil for 2 minutes, flip and cook for 1 minute more. Transfer to a plate.

2. Pour off the oil and return the skillet to the heat. Whisk in the butter and cook until the butter turns light brown and smells nutty. Add the wine and boil for 20 seconds. Add the lemon and parsley and boil for 20 seconds more. Season with salt. Pour butter over the sole and serve immediately.

Serves 2

The Squeamish American

TOM PERROTTA

Tom Perrotta is the author of Little Children *and* Election. *His most recent novel is* The Abstinence Teacher.

We all know one of those extreme eaters, the friend who travels to exotic places and performs the gastronomic equivalent of running with the bulls. These people live for the goat's eye, the snake's heart, the putrefying cheese, the crispy insect. I'd like to be one of them, but it's not gonna happen.

I am, I'm sorry to say, a very timid eater. The list of ordinary foods I can't bring myself to consume is long and depressing—milk, raw tomatoes, mushrooms, raisins, tofu, all sorts of fruits and a panoply of nutritious vegetables, not to mention everything that swims in the earth's rivers and oceans. I'm the kind of person who goes to Maine despite the fact that lobster is widely available.

As a child, I scandalized my Italian grandmother by regularly bringing a can of Campbell's chicken noodle soup to her house so I wouldn't have to eat any of the supposedly-delicious-but-somehow-troubling dishes she'd so lovingly prepared. I remember the wounded looks she used to give me as I slurped my industrial noodles and broth while everyone else at the table chowed down on baked ziti and braciola that tasted like the old country.

These days I'm pretty much resigned to my limitations. When I was in college, though, I really did try to do better. Accepting the challenge of my liberal education, I vowed to embrace new experiences—I went to Chinese restaurants, nibbled on brussels sprouts and kimchi, even sampled some sashimi. This project came to a head the summer after my junior year, when I traveled to Europe for the first time.

I arrived in Paris wide-eyed and full of optimism. Here I was! A whole new continent! Anything was possible! I had arranged to spend that first night with my friend Greg, who was apparently having a hard time making ends meet: he informed me as soon as I arrived that he'd spent his last franc on some eggs so that he could whip up a big omelet for our dinner.

Did I mention that eggs are a problem for me? I object to them so strenuously that I don't eat eggplant simply because it contains the word "egg" in its name. I knew I'd be tested in Europe; I just didn't expect it to happen so soon. It seemed ridiculous, somehow, traveling across an ocean only to find myself staring down at such a familiar and daunting nemesis.

I tried, I really did. The first bite went down okay—it always does. It's the second one that kills me. I want to swallow, but the food just sits there, moist and unwelcome, and I start to panic: Eggs. My mouth is full of eggs. Smiling at Greg, I reached for my napkin and made a big show of wiping my lips. I did this after every bite. My first night in Paris, and I spent it with half an omelet in my pocket.

It was a serious setback, and it established the tone for the rest of my trip. Somehow Europe wasn't what I'd expected. I went to the famous museums and walked down the legendary streets, but I remained stubbornly untransformed. I felt this keenly in West Berlin, where I stayed for a couple of weeks with a lovely family, settling into a routine there that felt a little too much like my life at home. Even the food seemed familiar; Frau H. kindly made sure I had peanut butter to spread on my brötchen every morning, and I ate a lot of sausage.

Hoping to shake things up, I went to East Berlin. After the thrill of crossing the border wore off, I found myself in the grip of another letdown. Yes, I was behind the Iron Curtain, but so what? I was still just a tourist—I could visit the propaganda museums and enter the grocery stores that sold nothing but orange soda, but I wasn't really learning anything, just confirming my preconceptions.

On my way to the train station, I decided to stop for a beer. I was escorted to a table already occupied by two uniformed East German soldiers and a civilian. They seemed pleased to meet me, and we downed a few steins. Feeling hungry and cheerful, I asked them in my terrible German accent if there was anything on the menu they might recommend, something local and authentic. All three immediately agreed—I should try the Hackepeter, a dish made of raw beef and chopped onions.

Maybe I was a little drunk, but I said yes. It helped that I actually liked raw meat as a kid—I often stole pinches of ground beef when my mother wasn't looking—and had nothing against onions. The waiter brought my meal, and I stared down at it in dismay—there was the meat, there was the chopped onion, and there, floating on top, was a raw egg, its yolk a viscous yellow sun.

The civilian, a guy named Klaus, helpfully mashed the concoction together with his fork, showing me how it was done. Once the egg had disappeared, a little of my courage returned. I poked my own fork into the sloppy mixture and took a tentative bite.

It was, I'm happy to report, quite tasty, a nice combination of blandness (the meat) and sharpness (the onion), with no eggy overtones whatsoever. I ate the whole thing. My new friends toasted my courage, and we proceeded to get quite drunk. When the soldiers left, I had a few more beers with Klaus, who grew somber and confessed to me that he was a dissident who'd been jailed several times for his political views. He invited me to return in a couple of days so that he could show me the real East Berlin, the places the government didn't want people to know about.

This was, of course, exactly what I was hoping for, a chance to experience something real and dangerous. On my second visit, Klaus took me to the wall and instructed me to take some pictures from the Western side that he could use to plan his escape. It's obvious to me now that he was working for the Stasi—no actual dissident would have been that stupid—but at the time I just felt frightened and confused. I promised him that I would mail him the pictures, but I knew I never would.

A few days later I had dinner on an American military base— my host was a woman from my hometown, the wife of a career officer. Over a meal of hamburgers and hot dogs, I told them of my troubling adventure with Klaus. The officer listened with increasing alarm and then told me I needed to go to the United States consulate the next day. At the consulate, I was informed that I might be vulnerable to arrest by the East German authorities for helping someone to escape. I protested that I hadn't actually helped Klaus, that I only made an insincere promise to do so, but this didn't seem to reassure anyone. It was strongly recommended that I leave the country in a sealed military train that couldn't be searched by the East Germans. Who was I to argue? I slipped out like a spook, missing out on a once-in-a-lifetime chance to experience the amenities of the East German penal system.

It was all because of the Hackepeter, and believe me, I learned my lesson. I don't eat raw meat anymore, nor do I ask the locals what they'd recommend. The rest of you can dine as adventurously as you like on fugu and roasted guinea pig. I'm going to stay home and open this can of soup. The broth is nice and salty, and the noodles are really soft.

"EGG"PLANT IN DISGUISE

2 tablespoons butter

3 tablespoons flour

2 cups milk

Salt and freshly ground black pepper

Grated nutmeg

About 6 tablespoons olive oil

2 pounds eggplant, cut crosswise into 1/3-inch slices

1 1/2 cups ricotta

2 teaspoons thyme leaves

1/2 cup grated Parmesan

1. Preheat the oven to 375 degrees. Make a béchamel: Melt the butter in a saucepan. When foamy, whisk in the flour and cook for 1 minute. Whisk in the milk, bring to a boil and simmer until thickened and smooth, 2 minutes. Season with salt, pepper and nutmeg. Cover and let cool.

2. Heat 2 tablespoons olive oil in a large nonstick skillet over medium-high heat. Add as many eggplant slices as will fit in one layer, season with salt and brown on both sides. Repeat with remaining oil and eggplant.

3. Fill the base of an 8-by-8-inch baking dish with 1/3 of the eggplant. Cover with 1/3 of the ricotta, followed by 1/3 of the béchamel. Sprinkle with thyme. Repeat two more times. Spread the Parmesan on top, and bake for 20 minutes. Place under the broiler for 1 minute to brown the top.

Serves 6

The Absolutely No-Anything Diet

GEORGE SAUNDERS

George Saunders, a 2006 MacArthur Fellow, is the author
of five books of fiction (including the short story collections
CivilWarLand in Bad Decline, Pastoralia, *and* In Persuasion
Nation) *and, most recently, the essay collection* The Braindead
Megaphone. *He teaches at Syracuse University.*

I was, of course, honored to be asked to write this essay on food, but also somewhat puzzled, since I completely ceased eating four years ago. Although the total cessation of eating has not always been easy—it's especially awkward, for example, when I'm invited to "go out to eat"—still, I believe I made the right choice.

There were a number of factors that led to my total cessation of eating.

First, I was tired of eating. I had begun to find eating monotonous. Always the same choices: what kind of dead animal, what sort of yanked-up vegetable/fallen fruit, in what manner would I like the cook to try to conceal the fact that I was eating one of the usual suite of dead animals/yanked-up vegetables/fallen fruits? Spices and seasonings had come to seem to me like the tools of a vast world lie.

Day after day, I found myself enacting the same cycle: eat, grow hungry, eat again. I began imagining my belly, filling and emptying, filling and emptying, imagined my mouth chewing and swallowing, chewing and swallowing. For hours at a time, when I should have been working, I sat in my cubicle, imagining my swollen belly and nutrition-engorged mouth, which is when, I recall, I first started skipping lunch.

Also, there were the moral issues. Every time I ate, I was aware that I was exploiting someone. The cow, yes, of course, the pig, the duck, but also the farmer, the trucker, the cook, the dishwasher and the waiter.

Frankly, with every bite, I felt more and more the oppressor. With every meal I don't eat, I am aware that somewhere a cow or pig, asparagus, broccoli, a waiter, etc., remains undisturbed. Sometimes, yes, when I drink, I still feel like an oppressor. Every time I drink, say, water, I am aware that I am exploiting the fish, the algae, the microorganisms, the men who built the pipeline, the filtration plant employees, the woman who made the glass from which I am drinking, the poor lackey who, stooping like a lowly indentured servant, brought me the glass of water.

I am hoping, soon, to discontinue drinking, but here I must admit to a certain moral timidity. I like to drink. I find it enjoyable. I especially like to drink alcohol. Perhaps it is some sort of compensatory mechanism, to offset the cessation of eating. I really don't know. I am not a psychologist. I only know that since I stopped eating, I have been drunk most of the time.

Here you may be thinking, Well of course he is drunk all the time; the poor morally pure thing has probably shriveled up to nothing from not eating and is therefore more susceptible to alcohol.

But no. The truth is, since I stopped eating, I have gained nearly seventy pounds.

Some may say, Well, this unfortunate weight gain must be related to his constant drinking. But no again. I didn't start getting constantly drunk until well after I had gained the seventy pounds and could barely fit into my pants. Last month I tried an experiment. I stopped drinking alcohol and drank only water, water that I got myself, very humbly, from the tap. I got it from the tap and skipped the oppressive glass stage altogether, taking the water directly into my cupped hands, bringing it meekly to my lips.

And guess what? I still gained ten pounds!

So, I thought, What the heck, and went back to drinking alcohol.

Needless to say, the total cessation of eating has not been easy. I think of food constantly. I think of great meals I have had in exotic foreign locations. I think of mediocre meals I have had in boring neutral locations. Lately, depressed by my weight gain, I have even found myself thinking of horrific inedible meals I have had in dangerously hostile places, where people were basically slapping the fork out of my hands while insulting me to my face.

But I know I must stay the course. Look at all the demons who ate! Hitler ate, Nero ate, Pontius Pilate ate, every murdering minor-league dictator and thieving banker in history ate. Now, I know what you're thinking: But good people ate, too! To which I would reply: Yes, but they ate less. Or, if they ate normal amounts, they enjoyed it less. Was Jesus a gourmand? I think not. Mother Teresa? Don't make me laugh. Gandhi? Always fasting.

Therefore, if less food is good, is not zero food better? If great moral beings have always chosen paths of minimal enjoyment, isn't the most righteous path no enjoyment at all?

Of late, we have become an aggressive and greedy nation. I believe that soon the pendulum will swing back, and we will become an ashamed, repentant nation. What better way to express our total self-loathing than to all stop eating at once, denouncing the endless cycle of intake and output, the corrupt global system of planting, harvest and feast? I will be happy to show the way.

What would help me is some company. Do you think, dear reader, you could join my movement? Will you, too, swear off the cruel oppression of eating? Will you, too, empty-bellied and clean-mouthed, join the ranks of the virtuous and ethereal, swelling inexplicably to tremendous righteous proportions, embarking on the greatest repentance of all, saying no to anything and everything that is in the least bit enjoyable?

If so, write me. I will respond during one of my brief sober periods and offer you some valuable advice on how to stop eating. Until then, I hope you will enjoy the following recipe:

LIGHT-AS-AIR BRUNCH

Air, approximately 6 cubic feet
1 pound highest-grade sirloin
3 eggs
4 perfect lobsters
Whipping cream, basil and the most expensive mushrooms obtainable
*   anywhere in the world*

1. Mix, in a mixing bowl, the air. Set aside to cool.
2. Take the sirloin, the eggs, the perfect lobsters and the incredibly expensive mushrooms and return them to the store.
3. Come home.
4. Remember that you also should have returned the stupid basil and the idiotic whipping cream.
5. Bag up basil and whipping cream, go back to the store exasperated, return basil and whipping cream, stomp out of store.
6. Come home, pretend to be eating the air in the bowl, look at

imaginary person to your right, slowly shaking head as if to say, Wow, was that good.

Serves 1 to 20

Important: If you experience actual pleasure during any of the above steps, you are doing it wrong. Smack yourself in the head with tenderizing mallet until headache develops, then repeat Steps 1 through 6, watching carefully for signs of enjoyment. A desirable variation involves skulking around the neighborhood to see if anyone is enjoying a lush, decadent meal. If so, lecture on benefits of self-denial and sinful nature of self-gratification until he or she loses appetite or chases you away. Sneak back later, firebomb his or her grill.

Discoveries

The Sixth Sense

GARY SHTEYNGART

Gary Shteyngart is the author of the novels Absurdistan *and*
The Russian Debutante's Handbook.

G rowing up, I dreamed of garlic the way some dream of
bright city lights. I had smelled the forbidden vegetable
(spice? herb?) during brief trips to Manhattan, roasted
garlic coating the poorer sections of town, clinging to the peeling
fire escapes, pouring down the tenement stoops to sucker-punch
me in the nose, my ten-year-old mind reeling with flavor and sum-
mertime heat and the still inchoate idea that sex could somehow
be linked with the digestive process (cf. *Seinfeld*).

Back home in sedated Little Neck, Queens, we feasted on Russian, or I should say Soviet, cuisine. Breakfast was a plate of roasted buckwheat groats with a puddle of butter soaking up the middle. Supper was a plate of thick, salty farmer cheese, sometimes with a can of peaches dumped on it, sometimes not. Around 3 p.m., a piece of boiled meat and some kind of wan vegetable were beaten into submission. "Please," I begged my mother, "if you let me eat only half a plate of buckwheat groats, I'll vacuum the whole house tomorrow. If we skip the farmer cheese, I'll give you back part of my allowance. I'll be supernice to Grandmother. Please, Mama, don't feed me."

I can't really blame my parents. They had spent the first half of their lives in the Soviet Union. They were doing their best. Roasted buckwheat was meant to ensure a beautiful, healthy organism. The nightly dose of farmer cheese was supposed to make you grow tall and strong. (I am five-foot-six on a good day.) Canned peaches were a sultry American luxury to be enjoyed at the end of a long working day. What was a form of punishment for me was for my parents a delicacy.

My first hint that food could be edible came at my grandmother's house. My grandmother loved me more than I loved myself, and on the occasions when I came to stay at her house after school, this love was expressed through a five-hour gorging process. While I reclined on a divan like a pasha, three hamburgers slathered with coleslaw and mustard were quickly brought to me. I ate them up with trembling hands as the Bionic Woman propelled her slender android limbs across the black-and-white 1950s television set and my grandmother peered turtle-like from behind the kitchen door, eyes wide with anxiety. "Are you still hungry, my beloved one?" she whispered. "Do you want more? I'll run to Queens Boulevard. I'll run to 108th Street. I'll run anywhere!"

"Run, Grandma, run!" I shouted. And Grandma would raise dust through Central Queens, her arms straining under the weight of pepperoni pizza pies, greenish pickle slices, cervelat smoked sausages from the Russian gastronom, ridged potato chips covered in some kind of orange crud, mayonnaise-heavy tuna fish salad from the kosher store, thick pretzels that I pretended to smoke like cigars, ranch dips that brought to mind only the barest hint of the garlic I craved, packets of creamy, chocolaty Ding Dongs. I ate and ate, trans fats clogging my little body, pockets of fat popping up in unlikely places, atop my ribs and at my sides. Sometimes I found Grandma in the kitchen dutifully sucking on a chicken bone. She supplemented her meager Social Security income by scrubbing toilets in a wealthier neighborhood nearby. She would have done anything to keep me in Ding Dongs.

And still it wasn't enough. The specter of garlic haunted me. I tried to name my need but could not. We lived in a Russian bland-food zone, where a visiting carne asada burrito would be promptly strip-searched and deported. We weren't poor, but we never went to restaurants, which my parents thought were only for fancy American millionaires like our favorite, J. R. Ewing of *Dallas*. He looked, as Grandma approvingly noted, upitanny. Extremely well fed.

The world beyond farmer cheese and kosher tuna began during my junior year of high school. I got an after-school job working for a Cuban guy who ran a moving company along with several more indeterminate industries. Most of our days were spent tearing down city streets in his car as he leaned out the window and shouted to passing women: "Hey, beau-tee-ful! You got a nice one! Don't deny it!" In the course of several years, we got lucky, let's say, never. Women were as mysterious to me as the piquant spices that never cluttered my mother's kitchen, so when my boss gave me coupons that could be redeemed for a meal at an expensive restaurant, I decided to take out two of the prettiest girls in high school. Girls and garlic: if only I could have both at the same time.

We began the evening by imbibing several rounds of Kahlúa followed by tequila slammers, and by the time we reached the TriBeCa restaurant, my companions and I were in fine form. Three hanger steaks and a bottle of sweet Frangelica liqueur later, the graceful sixteen-year-old brunette was loudly throwing up over the plush red banquettes. It was still the eighties; the dressy Wall Street clientele regarded us indifferently, gobbling up bland Maryland crab cakes with one hand while rubbing their raw, coked-up noses with the other. I felt that I was learning things, drawing a connection between fine dining and female companionship. But the food, as coolly professional as the Armani wearers around us, excited me no more than the storied groats of Little Neck. In the end, both the garlic and the girls got away.

I found what I was looking for one winter break from college in the early nineties at the corner of Horatio and Greenwich Streets. Against the genteel streetscape of redbrick town houses, the aroma of garlic, fresh, strong, unadulterated garlic, was weaving itself into the strands of my long hippie ponytail. My college friends and I had just been released, like wild animals, from the cold steel trap of a small Midwestern liberal arts college, where the dining hall grub was reputed to be only one grade above the food served in the state penitentiaries.

The restaurant was a Spanish place named El Faro, a Village stalwart where the likes of Dawn Powell and James Baldwin once dined. With the cozy look of a worn basement rec room, the ancient brown walls fading with murals of dancing señoritas and courting señores, Latin jazz on the speakers, the place was as warm as a companionable nineteen-year-old could hope for. We ordered two dishes (and in my many visits since I have tried no others): a mariscada in green sauce, a sizable pot filled with shrimp, scallops, clams and mussels coated in olive oil, parsley, onions and, yes, melting cloves of garlic; and shrimp al ajillo, saturated in garlic and hot sauce, perfect for scooping with fried Spanish potatoes or pouring over rice. My college girlfriend's pretty pale face turned red, my roommate embarked on a medley of satisfied mooing sounds, and my own tongue, barren for so long, accursed by the meager diet of my upbringing, was finally activated, letting the round strands of pure garlic dissolve in my mouth and making me feel, for the first time in my life, not like a duty-bound Russian immigrant and future earner but like a lusty, ravenous animal looking for satisfaction. I wanted to tell my companions that I loved them. I wanted to tell them that I was happy at last. I was not merely my parents' son but my own man, and although several more years of confinement at the Midwestern college remained, I would return to New York one day and take what was mine.

MARISCADA IN GREEN SAUCE

1/4 cup plus 2 tablespoons olive oil

1/4 cup plus 2 tablespoons finely chopped white onion

2 teaspoons minced garlic

1/2 cup finely chopped flat-leaf parsley

6 littleneck clams, washed

3 tablespoons flour

6 mussels, washed

24 medium shrimp, peeled and deveined

*12 bay scallops or 3 large sea scallops, quartered and tough muscle
  removed*

1/4 cup dry sherry

2 cups clam juice or unsalted fish stock

2 cups asparagus juice from two 15-ounce cans asparagus

Salt to taste

1. Place a large pot over medium heat and add the oil. Add the onion, garlic, parsley and clams. Sauté for 5 minutes.
2. Using a spoon, push the clams to one side, then sprinkle the flour into the base of the pot and stir to make a thin, smooth paste. One at a time, add the mussels, shrimp, scallops and sherry and simmer until the sherry evaporates, about 3 minutes. Pour in the clam juice or fish stock and the asparagus juice. Simmer until the mussels and clams are fully opened and the shrimp and scallops are opaque, about 5 minutes more. Season to taste with salt. At the restaurant, this is served in the pot and spooned over rice.

Serves 4

GAMBAS AL AJILLO
(SHRIMP WITH GARLIC)

1 cup olive oil

3 tablespoons crushed and chopped garlic

2 pounds medium shrimp, peeled and deveined

1 teaspoon hot red pepper flakes

1 teaspoon Tabasco or other hot sauce

1 teaspoon mild paprika

Salt to taste

1. Place a large pot over low heat. When the pot is hot, add the olive oil and garlic. Cook until the garlic has softened in the oil, about 2 minutes. Raise the heat to high and add the shrimp. Sauté for 2 minutes.
2. Sprinkle in the pepper flakes, Tabasco and paprika. Season with salt to taste. Cover, reduce heat to low, and cook until the shrimp is opaque and firm, about 5 more minutes. Taste and adjust seasoning, adding more Tabasco or red pepper flakes if you like more heat. Serve with fried potatoes or rice.

Serves 6

Recipes adapted from El Faro.

The Dining Room Wars

R. W. APPLE JR.

R. W. Apple Jr. (1934–2006) was an associate editor of the New
York Times. *He began working for the paper in 1963.*

I see by the newspapers that a bunch of eggheads have decided
that we form our tastes and appetites while we are still in
our mothers' wombs. Well, I've been a big, hungry boy for
as long as I can remember, so I guess my mother is to blame. Or
maybe my German-American grandmother, who had more talent
than money (just what you need to be a really good cook), and her
hearty hasenpfeffer and sauerkraut.

Wandering the world for the *New York Times* and other semi-
willing underwriters of my proclivities has given me the chance
to sample and resample and resample—okay, to gorge upon—the

best that San Francisco and New Orleans, Paris and Venice and London, Hong Kong and Kyoto have to offer. My thanks go to all the numbers crunchers who have made my education possible. But what, people constantly ask me, what about those jolly days in Fargo and Salt Lake City during campaign years, and what about Lagos and Moscow and wartime Saigon?

Not much fun, I grant you, from a culinary point of view. But a hungry boy always finds a way. As long ago as 1964, when I was a neophyte in national politics and a revolution in American cooking seemed as improbable as dietetic hot fudge sauce, I developed a fail-safe menu that worked even in the most gastronomically challenged precincts. Simple: dry martini, shrimp cocktail, New York strip medium rare, baked potato big as a shoe, maybe a few glasses of Gallo Hearty Burgundy.

Call me a cockeyed optimist if you like, but I've yet to find a country with nothing, absolutely nothing, that's worth eating or drinking. In Africa, I learned to count on Lebanese restaurants. I've forgotten the details of a thousand Lucullan French meals, but I vividly remember feasting on kofta (meatballs) at a joint in Monrovia. Nothing like good kofta after a week in the bush, I say. In a dozen or more flyspeck towns all over the world, I have subsisted nicely on Cantonese cooking that bore at least a nodding acquaintance with the real thing.

In Togo, as in all former German colonies, there is superb beer (though not sauerkraut, more's the pity). In Vientiane, Laos, starved for something crisp, I went berserk and ordered four helpings of celery—plain old garden-variety Pascal celery, but that night, in that place, it might have been foie gras. In cold-war Bulgaria, I was thrilled to discover that even the Communists couldn't ruin what was then, as now, the world's most sumptuous yogurt.

It helps that when it comes to food, I am neither High Church nor Low—or rather that I am both at the same time. I get as big a kick out of a good Chicago hot dog or Istanbul doner kebab as I do out of first-rate pheasant or Maine lobster.

Vietnam was a case in point. The Vietcong's unsporting habit of cutting the roads that connected Saigon with the countryside meant that only a pathetic trickle of first-class produce reached the capital, and that, in turn, meant that the sophisticated Vietnamese dishes that you eat today, there or elsewhere in the world, were out of reach. Somehow, though, there was always plenty of pho, the restorative, anise-scented beef or chicken noodle soup, delivered to your door for breakfast by frail-looking vendors, and that was ample compensation.

Moscow in the Brezhnev era presented a major challenge, met sometimes by improvident spending (forty dollars one depressing winter day for a delectable black-market cantaloupe from Georgia—the republic, not the state), but more often by toting. A dashing Italian correspondent struck up romances with flight attendants on Lufthansa, Alitalia and Air France planes, and he regularly landed in the Soviet Union laden with cheese, sweets and occasionally steaks that he was kind enough to share with less well-favored colleagues.

I myself sometimes returned to Moscow from sorties to the West with pockets filled with fruits and vegetables, like an Arcimboldo painting come to life.

But the staples of my days in the beneficent Russian capital were the luscious sour cream and unsurpassed rye bread, light and dark, available for a few cents a loaf, and caviar. The latter came by way of our hero, a black marketeer who toiled in the kitchen of the American Embassy snack bar. His product went well with the fine local firewater.

What I drank in Lagos and Saigon wouldn't have done much for Jancis Robinson or Hugh Johnson, but then context matters, right? In Nigeria, I laid in a stock of amusing Bulgarian white and unassuming Romanian red before the government clamped down completely on rummies like me. In Vietnam, I lugged Beaujolais in tin cans on combat operations. Not too bad, but the tropical heat didn't improve it much. The bottles of Tabasco that I carried in my fatigue pockets to doctor C rations fared better.

My insatiable urge to provide for myself has occasionally led me badly astray. Informed by an acquaintance in Saigon that for a measly few hundred piasters I could buy a case of Burgundy that had proved surplus to the French Embassy's requirements, I hastened to make the deal. The bottles were no doubt Burgundian, and the labels, too. The corks and even the capsules were intact. But some vile character had bored almost invisible holes in the punts and replaced noble wine with unspeakable swill.

During the revolution in Iran, we correspondents kept body and soul together with a daily lunch at Leon's Russian Grill, featuring borscht, double portions of caviar with blini and vodka. We knew it was the place to go because it was the favorite of all the best-connected spies in town.

Everything went well until the man himself, the fearsome Ayatollah Ruhollah Khomeini, finally returned to Tehran and decreed that no alcohol was to be served in the new Iran.

For my chum William Tuohy of the *Los Angeles Times* and me, this marked the end of civilized life as we had known it, but we figured we had to eat anyway, so we headed back to Leon's as usual on the first day of prohibition.

Our regular waiter pulled a long face when he saw us, carefully explained the new order of things and suggested 7UP as an appropriate alternative beverage. With heavy hearts, we agreed.

Resourceful fellows, those Iranians. When the bottles of "soda" arrived with our lunch—you must have guessed by now—they were filled with vodka.

LEBANESE KOFTA

1/2 cup grated fresh bread crumbs
1 cup Greek yogurt
2 garlic cloves, smashed and chopped

1 lemon, cut into 8 wedges
Salt and freshly ground black pepper
1 1/2 pounds ground lamb
1/4 teaspoon Turkish (Maraş Biber) red pepper
1/2 teaspoon cinnamon
1/3 cup finely chopped parsley
1/3 cup finely chopped onion

1. Heat a grill on high. Place the bread crumbs in a bowl and cover with water. Let sit for 10 minutes. In a small bowl, combine the yogurt, garlic and the juice of 2 wedges of the lemon. Season with salt and pepper. Set aside.

2. Drain the bread crumbs of water. Place the lamb in a large bowl. Top with bread crumbs, 1 teaspoon salt, Turkish pepper, cinnamon, parsley and onion. Mix with your hand until just combined. Form into logs, 6 inches long by 1 inch wide. Pierce lengthwise with a skewer. Grill on all sides until cooked through. Serve with the yogurt and the remaining lemon wedges.

Serves 6

I Scream

COLSON WHITEHEAD

Colson Whitehead's most recent book is the novel
Apex Hides the Hurt.

Mine is the story of a man who hates ice cream and of the world that made him.

I was once like you, always quick with a "Two scoops, please" and a "Whipped cream, damn it, whipped cream!" I loved a Breyers vanilla-chocolate-strawberry rectangle straight from the freezer. Never mind if it was a bit long in the tooth, nestled in there next to a half-empty bag of carrots-and-peas medley—scrape off the icy fur and it was good to go. Orange sherbet? Cool. In Baskin-Robbins, I used pure willpower to persuade the red digital lights of the Now Serving machine to announce my number, which was a sweat-smudged blob on the pink paper strip in my quivering hand. You can keep your Kiwi Mocha Bombasta: the nuclear green sludge of mint chocolate chip was as exotic as it got, and that's how I liked things.

Then I went to work in an ice cream store.

I started scooping at Big Olaf in 1985. Sag Harbor, on the East End of Long Island, was still early in its Hamptonization. Page Six couldn't find it on a map, Schiavoni's Market didn't stock sushi, and Billy Joel wasn't driving into trees. Perhaps Big Olaf was a harbinger. When it opened on Sag Harbor's Long Wharf, it made quick work of its nearby competitor, the Tuck Shop, which had been the town's long-standing ice cream joint. Big Olaf's secret weapon: the Belgian waffle cone, made before your very eyes. The smell of the batter haunts me still.

Most people think, Scooping ice cream, I could do that. But they don't understand the complexities, the high-stakes brinkman-ship of the modern-day ice cream industry. You had to memorize the names and ever-shifting locations of the trendy flavors, this week's double-chunk whatever. You had to learn the ropes of the toppings bar and become a bit of a cop in the process to keep the Heath Bars from rumbling with the gummy bears. You had to figure out a solid scooping technique, no matter what the cost. As a teenage boy, I was seized by a potent suspicion that my right arm was growing bigger than my left. You can imagine what chiseling ice cream all day was doing for my self-consciousness.

Don't get me started on the Tofutti. I'm never going back to that place.

Most of all, you had to master all things waffle. There was a bit of theater involved in the making of the cones. You sat by the door on a special perch so that everyone could see you while you ladled batter onto the four waffle grills, which were mounted together on a wheel. Spin the wheel, remove the cone, roll it up, add more batter, spin the wheel, and on to the next. Move too fast and the cones peeled off limp and useless; move too slow and they turned out brittle and crumbled to dust when you looked at them.

And all the while, the hungry masses in bright polo shirts and pleated khaki shorts watched your every move, a mob eager for this spectacle of cone process. The apparatus was probably leftover torture gear from some Belgian cold-war spy agency, unbolted from the floor of a basement interrogation room and shipped to the Hamptons. Where it found a home.

The perk of the job was all the ice cream you could eat, and ice cream was all I ate. There was a hot dog machine on-site, where the franks spun eternally like grisly, grim planets, and occasionally I'd make a wretched feast of one, but most of the time I ate ice cream. Chocolate in a plastic cup with rainbow sprinkles, chocolate shakes, chocolate ice cream sodas, chocolate twist dispensed by a lever into wavy, brown, short-lived peaks.

For breakfast and lunch, or lunch and dinner, depending on my shift. For three long summers.

I was nauseated at the end of each day, but I persisted, never suspecting that I was conditioning myself to hate that which I so ardently desired. My metabolism is such that I did not suffer any physical effects from my gluttony. I was cursed in other ways: in my aversion to ice cream, which spread quickly to most sweets, and then to all desserts.

When a person is offered dessert, a polite "I prefer not to" rarely does the trick. After hearing the details of how long my host labored over the apple brown betty, it's hard to refuse a bite. (Not so hard that I actually have some, but hard nonetheless.) There is a cost, I'm saying.

Birthday parties and weddings force me to share my tales of Olafian woe with my incredulous companions, who shake their heads before asking if they can have my plate. Take it, take it all. Most people mistake the terrified expression on my face in our wedding photos as a sign of regret. In fact, my face records the horror at the knowledge that I must eat cake at some point or, in the post-cutting photos, utter revulsion over the spongy clump of frosted hell scraping through my gut.

It is no small thing to remove yourself from the world of decent people. Predators abound. The natural enemies of the ice cream haters are the dessert fascists. You recognize them by the way they jab their little spoons at you from across the table, by the evangelical flourish with which they offer up their favorite phrases: "Have some," "You have to try this," "Trust me, you'll like it!"

Any resistance to their entreaties and they'll quickly turn on you. "How can you not like dessert?" they demand, and no excuse will calm these bullies. Your whole family could have been gunned down in some Ben & Jerry's massacre and they'll just wrinkle their noses and ask, "Not even one bite?"

To hate ice cream is to know dread at the clearing of the table, for at any moment the waiter will return with the dessert menu and put your nice evening to the test. Eventually you learn to compromise. Sometimes it is best to say, "I'll have a bite if you order something," and hope that your companions forget your promise. Most of the time they do—at the core of all dessert fascists is a frozen block of narcissism that will not melt. They don't want to share; they want affirmation of their choices.

Say what you will about ice cream haters—pity us, condemn us, take us off your guest list—but we don't need anyone's validation. We are content in ourselves, and at the feast of life, we happily dine alone.

Orange Crush

YIYUN LI

Yiyun Li is the author of A Thousand Years of Good Prayers,
a collection of short stories.

During the winter in Beijing, where I grew up, we always had orange and tangerine peels drying on our heater. Oranges were not cheap. My father, who believed that thrift was one of the best virtues, saved the dried peels in a jar; when we had a cough or cold, he would boil them until the water took on a bitter taste and a pale yellow cast, like the color of water drizzling out of a rusty faucet. It was the best cure for colds, he insisted.

I did not know then that I would do the same for my own

children, preferring nature's provision over those orange- and pink- and purple-colored medicines. I just felt ashamed, especially when he packed it in my lunch for the annual field trip, where other children brought colorful flavored fruit drinks—made with "chemicals," my father insisted.

The year I turned sixteen, a new product caught my eye. Fruit Treasure, as Tang was named for the Chinese market, instantly won everyone's heart. Imagine real oranges condensed into a fine powder! Equally seductive was the TV commercial, which gave us a glimpse of a life that most families, including mine, could hardly afford. The kitchen was spacious and brightly lighted, whereas ours was a small cube—but at least we had one; half the people we knew cooked in the hallways of their apartment buildings, where every family's dinner was on display and their financial states assessed by the number of meals with meat they ate every week. The family on TV was beautiful, all three of them with healthy complexions and toothy, carefree smiles (the young parents I saw on my bus ride to school were those who had to leave at six or even earlier in the morning for the two-hour commute and who had to carry their children, half-asleep and often screaming, with them because the only child care they could afford was that provided by their employers).

The drink itself, steaming hot in an expensive-looking mug that was held between the child's mittened hands, was a vivid orange. The mother talked to the audience as if she were our best friend: "During the cold winter, we need to pay more attention to the health of our family," she said. "That's why I give my husband and my child hot Fruit Treasure for extra warmth and vitamins." The drink's temperature was the only Chinese aspect of the commercial; iced drinks were considered unhealthful and believed to induce stomach disease.

As if the images were not persuasive enough, near the end of the ad an authoritative voice informed us that Tang was the only fruit drink used by NASA for its astronauts—the exact information my father needed to prove his theory that all orange-flavored drinks other than our orange peel water were made of suspicious chemicals.

Until this point, all commercials were short and boring, with catchy phrases like "Our Product Is Loved by People Around the World" flashing on screen. The Tang ad was a revolution in itself: the lifestyle it represented—a more healthful and richer one, a Western luxury—was just starting to become legitimate in China as it was beginning to embrace the West and its capitalism.

Even though Tang was the most expensive fruit drink available, its sales soared. A simple bottle cost seventeen yuan, a month's worth of lunch money. A boxed set of two became a status hostess gift. Even the sturdy glass containers that the powder came in were coveted. People used them as tea mugs, the orange label still on, a sign that you could afford the modern American drink. Even my mother had an empty Tang bottle with a snug orange nylon net over it, a present from one of her fellow schoolteachers. She carried it from the office to the classroom and back again as if our family had also consumed a full bottle.

The truth was, our family had never tasted Tang. Just think of how many oranges we could buy with the money spent on a bottle, my father reasoned. His resistance sent me into a long adolescent melancholy. I was ashamed by our lack of style and our life, with its taste of orange peel water. I could not wait until I grew up and could have my own Tang-filled life.

To add to my agony, our neighbor's son brought over his first girlfriend, for whom he had just bought a bottle of Tang. He was five years older and a college sophomore; we had nothing in common and had not spoken more than ten sentences. But this didn't stop me from having a painful crush on him. The beautiful girlfriend opened the Tang in our flat and insisted that we all try it. When it was my turn to scoop some into a glass of water, the fine orange powder almost choked me to tears. It was the first time I had drunk Tang, and the taste was not like real oranges but stronger, as if it were made of the essence of all the oranges I had ever eaten. This would be the love I would seek, a boy unlike my father, a boy who would not blink to buy a bottle of Tang for me. I looked at the beautiful girlfriend and wished to replace her.

My agony and jealousy did not last long, however. Two months later the beautiful girlfriend left the boy for an older and richer man. Soon after, the boy's mother came to visit and was still outraged about the Tang. "What a waste of money on someone who didn't become his wife!" she said.

"That's how it goes with young people," my mother said. "Once he has a wife, he'll have a better brain and won't throw his money away."

"True. He's just like his father. When he courted me, he once invited me to an expensive restaurant and ordered two fish for me. After we were married, he wouldn't even allow two fish for the whole family for one meal!"

That was the end of my desire for a Tangy life. I realized that every dream ended with this bland, ordinary existence, where a prince would one day become a man who boiled orange peels for his family. I had not thought about the boy much until I moved to America ten years later and discovered Tang in a grocery store. It was just how I remembered it—fine powder in a sturdy bottle— but its glamour had lost its gloss because, alas, it was neither expensive nor trendy. To think that all the dreams of my youth were once contained in this commercial drink! I picked up a bottle and then returned it to the shelf.

Michelin Man

JAMES SALTER

James Salter is the author of Light Years *and* A Sport and a Pastime. Life Is Meals, *which he cowrote with his wife Kay, was published in 2006.*

I n a sense, the connection between France and food began for me at the World's Fair in New York in 1939. The restaurant at the French Pavilion was one of the big hits of the fair. Everyone, including my parents, talked about it and the difficulty of getting a reservation. To the best of my knowledge, my father never tried.

When the fair closed in 1940, Henri Soulé, who had managed the restaurant, along with members of the staff, decided to stay in the United States and open a restaurant themselves. Le Pavillon, as it was predictably named, opened on Fifty-fifth Street, across from the St. Regis Hotel, in October 1941, just before Pearl Harbor. Dedicated to perfection, it not only survived the war but also reigned as the jewel of the city for thirty-odd years. It was expensive, of course, though the prices seem laughable today. Château Margaux 1929 was, at the time, $4.50 a bottle.

I never ate at Le Pavillon either, it turned out. Too perfect, too expensive, too social. The first French restaurant, to stretch the term slightly, I ever ate at was Longchamps, part of a chain, now gone, that catered to a middle-class clientele. Creamed spinach, dinner rolls served with an adroit fork and spoon, white tablecloths, quiet conversation, an occasional laugh. I had become an officer in the Air Force, and as such, after the war, I found my way to Paris in 1950, but it was a more or less hasty visit without culinary revelations, except that the girls in the nightclubs, after a night of insisting on bad, overpriced Champagne, liked to order pigeon, which was also overpriced, in the little restaurants familiar to them that, now famished, they took you to.

Four years afterward, I was stationed in Europe, and it is at this point that memories become more distinct. We went to Paris, my wife and I, a number of times and also to the South of France. There were incredible discoveries to be made. In Paris, on the Rue d'Amsterdam, there was Androuët, where everything on the menu was made from, or if necessary with, cheese. There was Les Halles and gratinée, and someplace where the waitresses were dressed as serving wenches and you ate Rabelaisian fare. There was the first steak au poivre and quenelles de brochet, and we ate at the Méditerranée on the Place de l'Odéon, unaware of distinguished patrons like Picasso and Jean Cocteau. We assumed that lobster à l'armoricaine was simply a French misspelling.

Let me just say that once you have been exposed to French cooking and French life, and they take, there is a long and happy aftermath. It's like knowing how to carve a turkey or sail a boat: it puts you a notch up. Of course, there is also Italy and all that. We cook from Marcella Hazan and *Cucina Rustica*, as well as others, but France is where Vatel, the maître d'hôtel for the Prince de Condé, fell upon his sword, his honor destroyed, when the fish did not arrive on time; where Taillevent, the most famous cook of the Middle Ages, rose from humble beginnings to actual nobility in the kitchen of Charles VI; and where Talleyrand, upon departing for Vienna in 1814 to negotiate for a defeated France at a congress of victors, told the king that he had more need of saucepans than of instructions.

Cuisine is regarded by the French as their rightful possession. Madame de Maintenon, mistress of Louis XIV, established the Cordon Bleu as a cooking school, to become over the centuries the most famous in the world. Julia Child was among its alumni. Madame de Pompadour, also a king's mistress, was taught in her youth that food was one of the essential ways to hold a man, and she is renowned for having made good use of both. It was at Paris restaurants like Le Grand Véfour and La Coupole (well, Coupole is technically a brasserie) that the great names of France were to be found. Governments were made at Lipp, it was said, but they fell at La Coupole.

Chinon, Chaumont, a small village near Grasse called Magagnosc, Villeréal, sometimes Paris—these are some of the places we, or I, have lived in France, usually in rented houses, sometimes borrowed ones. Borrowed apartments in Paris are the best, and the best guidebook, old and familiar as it may be, for me is the red Michelin. Others have their points, but the Michelin is solid, thick and reliable. When it was first published by the Michelin tire company in 1900 to identify gas stations, hotels and repair shops along the road, it had only twenty pages. Over the years it has become a veritable encyclopedia covering all the towns and cities in France with a hotel or restaurant worthy of any notice—name, address, telephone and fax numbers, category, price, specialties, dates open and on and on, even whether or not you can bring your dog. Dogs are usually allowed in restaurants in France and are almost always well behaved.

It was in the *Guide Michelin* that we found a restaurant, La Ripa Alta, in Plaisance, in southwestern France, one summer. It had been given a Michelin star, and the ranking was deserved. We had an excellent meal, and for dessert, figs, marvelously plump and tender, bathed in a smooth, faintly alcoholic liquid. When the owner and chef, Maurice Coscuella, came around to the tables afterward, we asked about the figs, how he had done them. The recipe was his own, he said, would we like it? I gave him a pair of drugstore eyeglasses I was reading the bill with in exchange.

FIGS IN WHISKEY

1 package dried figs, Turkish or Greek seem best
2 cups sugar
1 1/2 cups Scotch whiskey

Boil the figs for 20 minutes in about a quart of water in which the sugar has been dissolved. Allow to cool until tepid. Drain half the remaining water or a bit more and add the Scotch. Allow to steep a good while in a covered bowl before serving.

The restaurant in Plaisance is not listed in the current *Michelin*. I cannot imagine Monsieur Coscuella having fallen from one star to oblivion. I prefer to think he retired after years of honest work in the kitchen, but the guide does not give forwarding addresses.

Struggles

A Not-So-Simple Plan

PATRICIA MARX

Patricia Marx is the author of Him Her Him
Again The End of Him.

I am, let's face it, not the best eater. I don't like foods touching, I insist that meat, fish and even fowl be perilously rare, and I know how to say "sauce on the side" in five languages. When I was a kid, my diet consisted of American cheese slices that I would not eat unless they had been cut into pretty shapes. On my birthday, I was allowed to skip dinner.

But just because I don't eat doesn't mean that food hasn't been served in my house. I know this may seem really and truly odd to hear, but I, Patty, am no slouch in the kitchen. How is it that I know what kind of fare your standard human beings crave? Easy. They eat with gusto everything I decline. Butter is the chief component of all my recipes. And when preparing for others, I prepare with abandon. My rule of thumb: The serving size per person is in fact twelve to fourteen times that indicated by the recipe. Also, before committing to an ingredient, visit a multitude of greengrocers, out-of-the-way ethnic markets and vegetable stands to make sure that, say, the fiddlehead ferns are the best of their kind within a two-hundred-mile radius. If you must bolt up to Boston for your Bibb, so be it. I don't know about you, but I require perfection in a dinner party.

It is with everlasting mortification, therefore, that I tell you I once gave a dinner party that suffered a flaw. It happened many years ago, at a surprise party I'd been pressured into throwing for a former colleague of mine, even though (between you and me) I never liked her all that much. In general, I'm against surprise parties. To my way of thinking, the only word that should follow "surprise" is "attack." In this case, though, I had reason to believe that nobody would much mind, except, of course, me.

And so I rolled up my sleeves and began my usual dinner party drill: three months before the event, I phoned my mother to ask her what I should serve, and then she phoned her friend Chy to ask her what I should serve. My mother said Chy said how about corned beef, baked beans, an orange, watercress and pine nut salad, and for dessert crème caramel, and I said to my mother nah, this crowd isn't ready for brined meat, they are one bite away from pizza and soda, so my mother went back to Chy, and Chy went back to the drawing board. The next day, my mother called to say how about duck cassoulet and I said one of the guests doesn't eat anything with fewer than four legs. . . . A week later, she woke me in the middle of the night. I got it, she said over the phone—filet sandwiches on kaiser rolls! Yes, everybody's always going nuts for filet, I concurred, but won't the guests feel gypped if they don't get to use cutlery?

Eventually, Chy and my mother figured out the menu, with a little help from their friends Nancy and Mike. Nancy's strength is table settings and Mike has never thrown out an issue of *Gourmet*. The team proposed that I start with mushroom rolls and caramelized bacon, followed by crabmeat casserole and shrimp Lamaze (no, not a baby shellfish dish; Lamaze is a Russian-dressing-like sauce named for the manager of a Philadelphia hotel) accompanied by roasted fingerling potatoes and a salad of haricots verts, grape tomatoes and shallots with pistou. For dessert, chocolate bourbon cake. By now, we were down to the wire. Only two months before the guests were to arrive and there was so much to do: iron the napkins, consult with my sister-in-law about what kind of candy to order from Jagielky's in New Jersey, read every recipe ever written about every dish I'd be serving, and get a new slipcover for the armchair. Oh, maybe drive to Maryland to pick up the crab. Did I mention that I don't own a car?

Let us not relive the ice crisis, which, with a stroke of luck, resolved itself. Let us instead proceed to the night of the party.

While the mushroom rolls were shrooming in the oven, I called my mother to ask should I divide them in two or three, and my mother said hold on, I'll call Hilary. Hilary is a caterer who serves the kind of meal you'd like to cook at home but you don't have the time or the eight-burner stove, and I guess you probably don't have a staff of four to help either.

I'm happy to report that the irises looked stunning (I believe emphatically in monochromatic flower arrangements). The silverware I borrowed from my parents was glistening—so what if I had to go to Philadelphia to get it? The guests were deep in debate about the weather. So far, so flawless.

But where was the guest of honor? She was supposed to have arrived long ago. I telephoned her cousin, whose job it was to get the birthday girl here, and there was no answer. You could interpret this as a good sign, but I didn't. Somebody asked shouldn't we just start.

During hors d'oeuvres, another guest said something about the bubonic plague, which made me positive I had a shrimp problem. I paged my friend, an infectious disease specialist, who assured me, while examining a patient, don't worry about bacteria growing on shellfish—people don't eat enough bacteria anyway.

While I was insisting that everyone take home the leftovers or else, my mother called to find out how things were going. Almost perfect, I said, and my mother said Chy and I have worked out your next menu.

Should you be wondering, the shrimp, as far as can be determined, didn't kill anybody, and the reason the raison d'être of the party never showed up was that—oh, don't get me started on the cousin. Suffice it to say, next time I will make sure the team handles the surprise.

Incidentally, my mother read the above and wants you to know that Chy would say that the menu is not complete without dinner rolls and they must be soft so they don't crumb all over the house.

CARAMELIZED BACON

You can make this up to 3 days in advance. Keep in a tightly sealed container at room temperature. This is a dish that can't be ruined. You can freeze the leftovers. But why are there leftovers?

1 pound bacon
1 1-pound box light brown sugar (about 2 1/4 cups)

1. Go to a butcher and spend as much money as you have on very good bacon. Cut it into medium-thick slices, say, 3/16 of an inch.
2. Preheat the oven to 400 degrees. Line a large, rimmed cookie sheet with parchment paper. (You don't have to butter or oil the paper.) Dump a box of brown sugar into a big bowl. Light brown sugar is best, but if you want to use dark brown, I won't

stop you. Add enough drops of water (about 1/4 cup) so that the sugar becomes more than damp but less than soupy. Some bacon-caramelizers add a dash of cayenne pepper, but I think this makes the dish too nutritious.

3. Dredge the bacon in the sugar, one slice at a time. If the sugar isn't sticking to the bacon, add some more water to the bowl. (By the way, you won't use most of the sugar, but it's good to have extra to drag the bacon through.) Place the bacon strips on the paper. I then smear some sugar on top of the bacon, on the theory that if a little sweet is good, more is better.

4. Place the bacon in the oven. It's impossible for me to tell you how long to keep the bacon because it depends on whether you like it chewy or crisp. Some recipes tell you to keep it in the oven for 8 to 13 minutes per side, depending on the thickness of the bacon. I keep it in on the longer side. You should take yours out when it resembles the kind of bacon you would like to eat. Cut it into 1 1/2-inch triangles. Serve at room temperature.

Serves 8 to 10

MUSHROOMS ROLLS

8 tablespoons softened butter
1/2 pound mushrooms, chopped
2 tablespoons finely chopped chives

2 tablespoons finely chopped scallions

Salt and freshly ground black pepper

10 slices white sandwich bread—regular, not thinly sliced

1/3 cup sour cream

1/3 cup grated Parmesan cheese

1. Preheat the oven to 375 degrees. In a medium skillet, melt 2 tablespoons of the butter over medium heat. Add the mushrooms, chives and scallions and sauté until the mushrooms release water. Continue to cook until the water evaporates and the mushrooms are tender. Season to taste with salt and pepper.

2. Cut the crusts off the bread, and then roll each slice with a rolling pin so that it is really, really flat. Butter the bread heavily on the top side, and when I say "butter" I mean drown.

3. Spread the bread lightly with sour cream and then with a thin layer of the mushroom mixture. I use a spoon. You can use whatever you want. Roll the bread up so it looks like Pepperidge Farm Pirouette cookies (which are cylinders, for anyone who is unaware of this baked treat). Spread more butter on the bread and roll in the Parmesan cheese. Wash the goop off your hands. Arrange, seam side down, on a cookie sheet and put in oven until the rolls brown, 20 to 25 minutes. Cut each roll into three pieces. Serve hot (you can warm them up in the oven).

Serves 10, makes 30 pieces

SHRIMP LAMAZE (À LA PATTY)

3 pounds raw or cooked shrimp, peeled and deveined

1/2 cup mayonnaise

1/2 cup chili sauce

1/4 cup Indian relish, such as Heinz

1/2 of a jarred or canned pimento, chopped

1/4 green pepper, diced

1 teaspoon finely chopped scallions

2 tablespoons finely chopped celery

1 tablespoon white wine vinegar

1 tablespoon mustard

1/8 teaspoon paprika

1/4 teaspoon freshly ground black pepper

1 teaspoon A.1. sauce or Worcestershire sauce

1 hard-boiled egg, diced (optional)

If using raw shrimp, parboil them. Put all the other junk together and add it to the shrimp. Stir gently. Do not use too much sauce, please! Just enough to coat the shrimp. Promise?

Serves 10 to 12

The Sauce and the Fury

JULIA CHILD WITH ALEX PRUD'HOMME

Julia Child was the author, with Louisette Bertholle and Simone Beck, of Mastering the Art of French Cooking *and the host of* The French Chef. *She died in 2004. Alex Prud'homme, Childs's nephew, is the author of* The Cell Game. *This story is an excerpt from* My Life in France, *by Julia Child with Alex Prud'homme.*

By late 1950, I felt ready to take my final examination and earn my diplôme from the Cordon Bleu in Paris. But when I asked Mme. Brassart, the school's director, to schedule the test—politely, at first, then with an increasing insistence—my requests were met with stony silence. The truth is that Mme. Brassart and I got on each other's nerves. She seemed to think that awarding a student a diploma was like inducting them into some kind of secret society; as a result, the school's hallways were filled with an air of petty jealousy and distrust. From my perspective, Mme. Brassart lacked professional experience, was a terrible administrator and tangled herself up in picayune details and politics. Because of its exalted reputation, the Cordon Bleu's pupils came from all over the globe. But the lack of a qualified and competent head was hurting the school—and could damage the reputation of French cooking, or even France herself, in the eyes of the world.

I was sure that the little question of money had something to do with Mme. Brassart's evasiveness. I had taken the "professional" course in the basement rather than the "regular" (more expensive) course upstairs, which she had recommended; I never ate at the school; and she didn't make as much money out of me as she would have liked. It seemed to me that the school's director should have paid less attention to centimes and more attention to her students, who, after all, were—or could be—her best publicity.

After waiting and waiting for my exam to be scheduled, I sent Mme. Brassart a stern letter in March 1951, noting that "all my American friends and even the U.S. ambassador himself" knew I had been slaving away at the Cordon Bleu, "morning, noon and night." I insisted that I take the exam before I left on a long-planned trip to the United States in April. If there was not enough space at the school, I added, then I would be happy to take the exam in my own well-appointed kitchen.

More time passed, and still no response. I was good and fed up and finally spoke to Chef Bugnard, my professor, about the matter. He agreed to make inquiries on my behalf. Lo and behold, Mme.

Brassart suddenly scheduled my exam for the first week in April. Ha! I continued to hone my technique, memorize proportions and prepare myself in every way I could think of.

On the big day, I arrived at the school, and they handed me a little typewritten card that said, "Write out the ingredients for the following dishes, to serve three people: oeufs mollets; côtelettes de veau en surprise; crème renversée au caramel."

I stared at the card in disbelief.

Did I remember what an oeuf mollet was? No. How could I miss that? (I later discovered that it was eggs that have been coddled and then peeled.) How about the veau "en surprise"? No. (A sautéed veal chop with duxelles, or hashed mushrooms, on either side, overlaid with ham slices and all wrapped up in a paper bag— the "surprise"—that is then browned in the oven.) Did I remember the exact proportions for caramel custard? No.

Zut alors, and flûte!

I was stuck, and had no choice but to make everything up. I knew I would fail the practical part of the exam. As for the written exam, I was asked how to make fond brun, how to cook green vegetables and how to make sauce béarnaise. I answered them fully and correctly. But that didn't take away the sting.

I was furious at myself. There was no excuse for not remembering what a mollet was or, especially, the details of a caramel custard. I could never have guessed at the veau en surprise, though, as the paper wrapping was just a lot of tomfoolery—the kind of gimmicky dish a little newlywed would serve up for her first dinner party to épater the boss's wife. Caught up in my own romanticism, I had focused on learning far more challenging fare—filets de sole à la Walewska, poularde Toulousaine, sauce Vénetienne. Woe!

There were no questions about complicated dishes or sauces, no discussion about which techniques and methods I'd use. Instead, they wanted me to memorize basic recipes taken from the little Cordon Bleu booklet, a publication written for beginner cooks that I had hardly bothered to look at. This exam was far too simple for someone who had devoted six months of hard work to cooking school, not to mention countless hours of her own time in the markets and behind the stove.

My disgruntlement was supreme, my *amour-propre* enraged, my bile overboiling. Worst of all, it was my own fault.

I despaired that the school would ever deign to grant me a certificate. Me, who could pluck, flame, empty and cut up a whole chicken in twelve minutes flat! Me, who could stuff a sole with forcemeat of weakfish and serve it with a sauce au vin blanc such as Mme. Brassart could never hope to taste the perfection of! Me, the supreme mistress of mayonnaise, hollandaise, cassoulets, choucroutes, blanquettes de veau, pommes de terre Anna, soufflé Grand Marnier, fonds d'artichauts, onions glacées, mousse de faisan en gelée, balantines, galantines, terrines, pâtés, laitues braisées . . . me, alas!

Later that afternoon, I slipped down to the Cordon Bleu's basement kitchen by myself. I opened the school's booklet, found the recipes from the examination—oeufs mollets with sauce béarnaise, côtelettes de veau en surprise and crème renversée au caramel— and whipped them all up in a cold, clean fury. Then I ate them.

OEUFS MOLLETS, SAUCE BÉARNAISE (SOFT-COOKED EGGS, BÉARNAISE SAUCE)

6 very fresh eggs
Salt

FOR THE BÉARNAISE SAUCE
4 peppercorns, crushed
1 large shallot, chopped
3 tablespoons chopped fresh tarragon
2 tablespoons white wine vinegar
1/4 cup white wine
2 egg yolks
2 tablespoons water
8 ounces unsalted butter, melted
1 tablespoon chopped fresh chervil
Cayenne pepper

1. Prepare the oeufs mollets: Cook very fresh eggs in boiling, salted water for 5 to 6 minutes, according to the size. Transfer to a bowl of cold water to stop the cooking. Peel the cooled eggs under warm running water and set aside in a bowl of hot, not

boiling, salted water until ready to serve. "Mollet eggs" can be kept warm for some time without the yolks hardening.

2. Prepare the béarnaise sauce: Combine the crushed peppercorns, shallot, 2 tablespoons of the tarragon, the vinegar and the wine in a small heavy-bottomed saucepan. Bring to a boil and cook over low heat until all the liquid has evaporated. Remove from the heat, cool and strain.

3. Put the egg yolks, the water and the cooled reduction in a medium saucepan. Whisk over very low heat until the mixture becomes foamy and thickens and the whisk leaves a clear trail on the bottom of the pan. Do not let the mixture boil. Remove from the heat.

4. Whisking constantly, add the melted butter, drop by drop, until the mixture starts to emulsify. Then whisk in the remaining butter in a slow steady stream until the sauce is thick and creamy. Whisk in the chopped chervil and the remaining tablespoon of tarragon. Season to taste with salt and cayenne pepper. Serve spooned over the eggs.

Serves 6

CÔTELETTES DE VEAU EN SURPRISE
(VEAL CHOPS SURPRISE)

11 tablespoons unsalted butter
2 large shallots, finely chopped
10 ounces mushrooms, trimmed, rinsed, dried and finely diced

Salt and freshly ground black pepper
6 veal chops, trimmed, 6 ounces each
2 tablespoons vegetable oil
12 thin slices cooked ham
1 egg white, beaten

1. Heat 3 tablespoons of the butter in a large skillet over low heat. Add the shallots and sauté until softened. Increase the heat to high and add the mushrooms. Season with salt and pepper. Sauté until all the moisture has evaporated, then spread the mixture on a plate to cool.

2. Heat the oven to 400 degrees. Season both sides of the chops with salt and pepper. Heat the oil and 1 tablespoon of the butter in a large skillet over high heat. Add the chops and brown lightly on both sides. Transfer to paper towels to drain, and pat dry.

3. Cut six 12-by-10-inch rectangles of parchment paper. Melt the remaining 7 tablespoons butter. Position a rectangle of parchment so that the 10-inch side is directly in front of you. Brush with butter, and place a tablespoon of the mushroom mixture in the middle of the lower half of the rectangle. Top with a slice of ham, topped with a veal chop. Cover the veal with another slice of ham and another tablespoon of mushrooms. Repeat with the remaining pieces of parchment paper, veal chops, mushrooms and ham.

4. Brush a 1/4-inch border of egg white along the 3 edges of the lower half of the rectangles. Fold the upper half of the rectangle

over the veal, and align the edges. Again brush the 3 edges with egg white, then fold and crimp the edges to make a strong seal. Continue until all six chops are encased in parchment. Brush the surface of the parchment with the remaining melted butter, and brush the crimped edges again with egg white. Lay the veal packets on a baking sheet and bake until the packets are puffed and brown, about 15 minutes. Transfer each packet to a plate to be opened at the table.

Serves 6

CRÈME RENVERSÉE AU CARAMEL
(CARAMEL CUSTARD)

1/2 cup plus 2/3 cup sugar

2 cups milk

1 1/2 teaspoons vanilla extract

2 large eggs

4 large egg yolks

1. Preheat the oven to 350 degrees. In a small saucepan, combine 1/2 cup sugar with 1/4 cup water. Bring to a boil over low heat, stirring to dissolve the sugar. Increase the heat to high and cook, without stirring, until the syrup turns a light caramel color. Remove the saucepan from the heat and dip the bottom into cold water to stop the cooking. Pour the caramel into a 4-cup

charlotte mold, and tilt so that it covers the bottoms and sides. Let cool.

2. In a small saucepan, bring the milk and vanilla to a boil. In a heatproof bowl, beat the eggs, egg yolks and 2/3 cup sugar until blended. Whisking constantly, pour the hot milk into the egg mixture; let rest for a few minutes, then strain. Pour the custard into the caramel-coated mold.

3. Put the mold in a small but deep baking or roasting pan, and add hot water to come about two-thirds up the sides of the mold. Place the pan on the stove over medium heat, and bring the water to a simmer. Transfer the pan to the oven. (The water should stay at a low simmer at all times; do not let it boil or the custard will overcook.) Bake until a knife inserted into the center of the custard comes out clean, 40 to 50 minutes. Keep the custard in the baking pan until the water cools. Remove from the pan to finish cooling. To serve, run the tip of a knife around the top of the custard to loosen it. Invert a serving platter over the mold and quickly turn it over again. Carefully remove the mold.

Serves 6

All recipes adapted from Le Cordon Bleu.

Bean There

TUCKER CARLSON

Tucker Carlson is an anchor for MSNBC in Washington.

I bet we were the only people in my neighborhood growing up who ate B&M baked beans. We lived in La Jolla, California, twenty-five miles north of the Mexican border, where the only beans you saw were refried or served in salad. B&M beans came in a can, suspended in molasses with a chunk of salt pork. They seemed like the sort of thing you'd eat by the woodstove if you were snowbound in the mountains. They were a little heavy for La Jolla.

That was doubtless the appeal for my father, who came from

New England and ate things like shepherd's pie, rhubarb and other mysterious foods that baffled guacamole-stuffed Southern California natives like my brother and me. But we ate the beans anyway, partly out of respect for my father, but also because they were delicious. In the summers, on the way from the Boston airport to vacation in Maine, we'd salute as we drove past the immense brick B&M plant in Portland. I remember wondering who worked there.

One summer during college, I found out. My roommate and I were living in Portland, though not very successfully. I'd applied to Denny's; he'd put his name in for a bartending job. Neither of us heard back. We sold car insurance door to door for a day. Finally we tried a temp agency. The next afternoon we found ourselves wearing white uniforms and hairnets and reporting for duty at the Burnham & Morrill baked bean factory.

B&M was a strict union shop, closed to all but members of the Bakery, Confectionery, Tobacco Workers and Grain Millers International, local 334, and possibly their sons and nephews. But for some reason that summer the union allowed an exemption for temporary help. We went to work on the second shift at $6.60 an hour.

The B&M plant was built in 1913 and, from what I could tell, hadn't been updated since. Outside, the building was dominated by a towering brick smokestack that belched bean fumes into the salty Portland air. Inside, it was a time capsule. True to advertising, B&M's beans (white pea and red kidney) were cooked as they had always been, in enormous cast-iron pots that were lowered into brick ovens. The pots hung from chains and moved across the plant floor on steel rails suspended from the ceiling.

It looked to me as if someone must have bribed the safety inspectors. Each bean pot was the size of a Fiat. They whipped across the floor at surprisingly high speeds, often pushed by workers who looked as if they could have used a nap. (When your shift starts at four in the afternoon, there's ample time to drink before work.) Occasionally a pot would slip the rails and come crashing down. I saw it happen once. The impact sounded like a massive explosion. During our next smoke break, one of my gossiping coworkers claimed that the Burnham & Morrill plant had the highest rate of work-related injuries in all of Pet Inc., then the corporate parent. I believed him.

Most of my jobs were safe enough. One week I scraped charred beans from the insides of the ovens. The next I ran a machine that stacked cans onto pallets. For two weeks after that, I extracted the hot cans in which B&M baked its brown bread. They were made in enormous pressure cookers that looked like missile silos and were called reefers, for some mysterious reason. By the end, I got curious about the bread and tasted some. Surprisingly, it was pretty good.

By July I'd been assigned to a pot-saucing station, mixing ingredients for 16- and 18-ounce containers of barbecue-flavored pea beans. For each pot we combined 21 gallons of hot water with 4.3

ounces of mustard slurry, a portion of ground bacon and 8 ounces of liquid hickory-smoke flavor. I was the liquid-hickory man.

Until that day, I'd naïvely imagined that food ingredients resembled food. Not so with barbecue sauce (i.e., liquid-hickory flavor). The flavor came in white plastic 50-gallon drums, shipped from a chemical plant in New Jersey. I learned right away that you didn't want to get the flavoring on your skin. It was the consistency of oil-based deck sealant and harder to remove. Within an hour every one of my fingers was dyed a deep yellow, the color of nicotine stains. I looked like a wino with a bad Pall Mall habit.

But at least I wasn't bored. The women on the pork line clearly were. I walked by them several times a day as they stood silently at a conveyor belt, dropping pieces of salt pork into cans of beans, one piece per can, eight hours a day. The monotony was enough to make you hope for a falling bean pot.

One day toward the end of my short career at the plant, a supervisor sent me to a storeroom on the third floor. Inside there was a pile of hundreds of bean cans, all of them full. Apparently some of these cans had bad seams. It was impossible to know exactly which ones were defective, but the company wasn't taking chances. Leaky seams meant spoiled product, maybe even botulism. You couldn't just throw them away, for fear that someone would retrieve them from the trash, eat them, get sick and sue. They had to be destroyed. My job was simple: puncture every can.

The assignment came with a special tool, fabricated in the

millwright's shop. It looked like a framing hammer with a steel spike welded to the end. It made a satisfying sound as it pierced the cans.

I had a great time for the first hour. Then I came to a bad can. I should have known what it was. It looked different from the others, misshapen and bulging in the middle. If you've ever shot a can of shaving cream with a BB gun, you know what happened next. A plume of fermented beans burst forth like a geyser. The liquid was brown and bubbling and smelled like sewer gas. It hit me directly in the face, spraying into my eyes and mouth, and running down the inside of my collar. I felt like screaming, but there were people watching, so I just kept whacking cans. My uniform stuck to me for the rest of the night.

On my final day of work, I stopped by the company store to pick up some beans, which B&M sold to employees at cost. Cheap beans were considered a key perk of the job, and in fact they were. The labels were often flawed and the cans dented, but the beans were fine, and incredibly inexpensive. For three dollars, I bought a case of pork-free pea beans in sauce. I threw it on the backseat of my car and drove off.

Last year I was rooting through a cabinet in the laundry room of our summer house looking for Fourth of July fireworks. There, next to a leaky container of Tide, were the beans. I'd bought them fully intending to cook them for dinner. Tastes change over time, though. I worked there in 1989. I haven't had a baked bean since.

BOSTON BAKED BEANS

The trick to good baked beans is cooking them very slowly with indirect heat. This recipe by James Beard calls for baking them in a tightly sealed casserole in an oven barely hot enough to toast bread. As the hours pass, the beans drink up a broth flavored with brown sugar (or molasses), mustard and pepper. The gentle cooking prevents the beans from breaking up and becoming mushy. By the time they're done, the pork is falling off its bones and the beans are the classic rusty brown. Be sure to season them amply with salt so the sweetness has a sturdy counterpart.

Beard's recipe calls for dark brown sugar. The alternative is to use molasses, which will render a final flavor and color more familiar to canned-bean devotees. The recipe itself requires no great cooking skills—if you can peel an onion and boil water, you're all set—but it will easily take up an afternoon. Plan it for a day when you're at home.

2 cups of dried white pea beans (navy beans)

1 scant teaspoon salt, plus more to taste

1 medium onion, peeled

4 pork spareribs, or 8 baby back ribs

1/3 cup packed dark brown sugar or molasses

2 teaspoons dry mustard

1 teaspoon freshly ground black pepper

1. In a large bowl, soak the beans in 2 quarts of water for 6 hours. Drain the beans and put them in a large pot. Add the salt and enough cool water to cover 2 inches above the beans. Bring to a boil, then lower the heat and simmer gently, stirring occasionally, until the beans are just barely tender, 30 to 40 minutes. Drain well.

2. Bring another pot of water to a boil. Preheat the oven to 250 degrees. In the bottom of a large casserole with a tight-fitting lid, place the peeled onion—yes, whole—and spareribs (or baby back ribs). Spread the beans on top. In a small bowl, mix together the brown sugar (or molasses), mustard and black pepper and add this to the beans and pork. Pour in just enough boiling water to cover the beans, put the lid on and bake, occasionally adding more boiling water to keep the beans covered, until they are tender but not falling apart, 4 to 5 hours.

3. Remove the casserole from the oven. Season the beans with salt. Pull the meat from the ribs. Discard the bones and excess fat and stir the meat back into the beans. With the lid off, return the casserole to the oven and let the beans finish cooking, uncovered and without additional water, until the sauce has thickened and is nicely caramelized on top, about 45 minutes more.

Serves 6

Adapted from *The James Beard Cookbook*, by James Beard.

Home Turf

KIRAN DESAI

Kiran Desai is the author of Hullabaloo in the Guava Orchard *and* The Inheritance of Loss.

One morning, we heard a shriek from the kitchen. Our cook, Saratbhai, came racing to get my mother to view the evidence: my sister's handprint in the curd dish and a line of white plops all the way to the bedroom we shared.

"She has spent the curd, the limes, the cream, the almonds, the eggs, the gram flour, the turmeric!" he screamed melodramatically. My beautiful sister, at eighteen, was in love with her own beauty, even as my parents advised her: "If you stare so much at yourself you'll think everyone is staring at you, too."

But she couldn't stop. To maintain that complexion despite the Delhi dust, to sustain the river sweep of hair that could have propelled the narrative of a fairy tale, she used homemade potions concocted from the kitchen supplies. Washed down the drains, they caused an outbreak of cockroaches.

Saratbhai came from a village on the Bengal-Orissa border that grew cashews and a life of rural poverty we couldn't imagine. Yet he was an expert in Indian, Chinese and Continental food and could make a kebab that brought back the glory days of the Mughals when kebabs were served with poetry and an extravagance of etiquette. Or he could concoct Irish stew with Marmite hearty enough to please the stubbornest Anglophile when it was rainy and it was just the stew, the Jane Austen and you.

The more the emotional facets of our own experiences became linked to Saratbhai's cooking, the more our fear mounted that he would one day be stolen from us. My father would say, "The wife of that architect down the road, she's after Saratbhai, keeps smiling at him in the Mother Dairy milk line." Saratbhai was irreplaceable: he knew it, we knew it, he knew we knew it; and this gave him permission to indulge his contrariness.

His temper would be turned on us, for example, if we sampled the Cauliflower Manchurian at Chopsticks or mutton patties at the India International Center. He begrudged us anything but his own food; we returned home to sulking that turned to gloating laughter should we fall ill.

But the truth was that this contrariness hid his tenderness. To Saratbhai we sisters were Tanibaby and Kiranbaby. It was during this time that I became a disciple of *The Landour Cookbook*. Compiled by American missionaries, it promised an easy path to the Wacky Crazy Cake.

In the afternoons, as the rest of the family slept the sodden sleep of a hot climate, I would tiptoe into the kitchen. Saratbhai would be napping on the even hotter rooftop, among the rows of earthenware pots he placed there to cool the concrete.

My mother was amused by this interest of mine. She preferred to spend her time among her books, a collection that traveled all the way from floor to ceiling. For an Indian woman, she displayed a lack of meddling in the kitchen that was remarkable and weird. Saratbhai boasted about it to the others in the community of harassed, bullied cooks. It gave him status. He was our kitchen deity.

But now his artistry was being snubbed by a child, by tastes from abroad that he could not gauge or understand, gleaned from a book he could not read. An uncertain world where West was better than Indian, where the young ridiculed the old—a world for which he didn't have skills to cope might pour into his kitchen, undo our home and his dignity within it.

"Are there any eggs?" I would ask Saratbhai. He would often play us sisters against each other, hoping the cook and the beauty queen would cancel each other out.

"Go look in Tanibaby's cupboard!"

"Honey?" Tani asked.

"Kiranbaby would know!"

At 4 p.m. he returned with the evening milk; hearing the *chup-chup-chup* of his Hawaii rubber slippers, I would run out fast as the heavy summer climate allowed, the yells trailing me: "How will I make dinner! Hoo! The raisins are spent! Hoo!"

When my cakes would turn to glue, he would dispose of the mess with grim triumph. Wasted eggs, wasted butter, wasted precious gray ration-shop sugar. I felt the same shame that I did when I stood before my father with the mathematics paper that came back with half a mark out of 100. But while I accepted the mantle of shame in mathematics, it was harder to be humiliated in the field of macaroons. For a while, I refused to succumb, even as Saratbhai began to hide the flour behind the gas tank, the oil behind the old newspapers.

Before I could cook, I had to go on a treasure hunt, my time further curbed, haste as poisonous for cooking as fear, of course.

Yet one day I tried a soufflé, excited by the illustration. It never did become a cloud; it never had a golden crown; it was dead at birth. The kitchen clock made a cartoon tick-tock: almost 4 p.m.

In fright, I emptied the sludge into a plastic bag and ran to the rooftop from where you could see our entire neighborhood. I whirled the bag about my head and threw it as far as I could.

Life was quiet for about twenty minutes . . . and then came Saratbhai. In one hand he had the milk can as usual, and in the other a sad bag dripping yellow. He was so angry he couldn't speak, his lips pressed together in a straight line to show I'd stepped over the limit. He had walked by that bag, and he had known in his bones—every instinct finely tuned for my betrayal—that he had found his belongings lying there violated and abandoned. After this, he carried the eggs up to bed with him in the afternoons. In fact, he removed half the larder after lunch and placed it under his mattress. Over the ingredients of his art, he slumbered in peace.

So I never made a soufflé. Instead, I returned to reading, and years later I became a writer sustained on store-bought baked goods (with a sister whose looks were sustained on store-bought potions). A writer whose work spilled over with food metaphors, long dinners and difficult cooks—as if she were still desperate to get into the kitchen.

SARATBHAI'S SHAMMI KEBABS

1 pound ground lamb
2 tablespoons mustard oil or vegetable oil (see Note)
6 green cardamom pods, seeds removed and ground, shells
   discarded
1 (1-inch) cinnamon stick
6 whole cloves
6 garlic cloves, minced

1 teaspoon grated ginger

2 medium onions, chopped

1 tablespoon yellow or red lentils

Pinch of mace

1 teaspoon freshly grated nutmeg

Salt

2 serrano chilies, seeded and finely chopped

1 teaspoon ground coriander

1 teaspoon cumin, toasted and ground

8 allspice berries, crushed and minced

1 tablespoon chopped cilantro

1 egg, beaten

2 tablespoons roasted chickpea flour (see Note)

Canola oil

1. In a saucepan, combine the meat, mustard oil, 2 cups of water, the ground cardamom seeds, cinnamon, cloves, garlic, ginger, onion, lentils, mace, nutmeg and 1/2 teaspoon salt. Boil over medium-high heat until all of the water evaporates, about 50 minutes. (When the water is nearly evaporated, stir constantly to prevent burning and help water evaporation.) Add the chilies, coriander, cumin, allspice and more salt to taste.

2. Remove the cinnamon and cloves. Transfer the meat mixture to a food processor and pulse until finely ground and uniform, but not completely smooth, about 15 times.

3. Return the mixture to the saucepan and cook over medium
   heat, stirring frequently, until the mixture is dry enough to hold
   together when pinched, about 15 minutes. Transfer to a bowl
   and let cool. Stir in the cilantro, egg and chickpea flour. Roll
   meat into tight balls, 1 1/2 to 2 inches in diameter, and gently
   press into patties. Pour a tablespoon or two of oil in a griddle
   or nonstick skillet and set over medium heat. When hot, brown
   the kebabs, about 1 minute per side. (The kebabs are delicate;
   flip them gently.)

   Serves 4, makes 12 kebabs

Note: Mustard oil and roasted chickpea flour are available at
Patel Brothers, 37-27 74th Street, Jackson Heights, Queens, (718)
898-3445; Kalustyan's, 123 Lexington Avenue, Manhattan, (212)
685-3451.

TOMATO-GINGER-RAISIN CHUTNEY

1 (14-ounce) can crushed tomatoes
1 (3-inch) piece of ginger, peeled and grated
3 garlic cloves, crushed
1 tablespoon sugar
1 teaspoon tamarind paste or white wine vinegar
Pinch of chili powder

1/4 teaspoon salt, plus more to taste

1/3 cup raisins

Combine all of the ingredients in a small saucepan and simmer gently over low heat, stirring occasionally, until the mixture reaches a chutney consistency, 30 to 40 minutes. Season to taste with salt. Cool and serve with kebabs.

Makes 1 1/4 cups

Line of Sight

GABRIELLE HAMILTON

*Gabrielle Hamilton is the chef and owner of Prune
in New York City's East Village.*

A couple of years ago I placed an ad for a line cook. And there was a guy who, according to his résumé, should have been right up my alley. He held a grill position in a busy seafood joint at the shore; he had studied philosophy and political science; and he had about four years of experience in the industry. I was looking forward to meeting this guy, with whom an after-work conversation over beers might be possible, and who had just enough years in the industry to still have something to learn, but not so few that he would need to be taught everything.

I called him up and we had a pleasant phone exchange. I liked his voice, his manner; he was intelligent and articulate. I invited him in for an interview the following day.

The first thing I noticed when he arrived was that he was blind. His eyes wandered around in their sockets like tropical fish in the aquarium of a cheap hotel lobby.

We managed a handshake and sat at the bar and I asked him about his responsibilities at the busy seafood restaurant, and he answered entirely reasonably. He understood the language I used and spoke it back to me: the sort of shorthand code that people who work in kitchens speak.

I said, "How many covers for lunch?"

And he said, "Eighty-five to one hundred ten."

I said, "What kind of mise"—prep—"is there in a fried seafood place?"

And he laughed and said, "Yeah, it's all lemon wedges and tartar sauce."

We talked a bit about his education in philosophy: he was a Hegel fan. Finally, I showed him our menu. He held it up to his face as if to breathe in its written contents, to discover by inhaling what it said in plain print. I felt more certain than ever when I observed this that he was blind, but naturally doubted myself because obviously the guy had worked in restaurants, something that—though we may joke—really can't and shouldn't be done. And in spite of the proximity to his face at which he held the menu,

I thought maybe I was making some despicable assumptions about the "sight-impaired" and needed to get my politics up to date. So I booked him for a "trail," the industry equivalent of an audition.

I went right downstairs and unpinned the schedule from the corkboard and penciled him into the grill station the next night. He wrote his new phone number on the top of his résumé in large unwieldy script and even managed, more or less, to locate and cross out the old number. I looked at him as directly in the eyes as I could, thinking maybe I should ask about what seemed obvious, but instead I said: "Well, you seem average in build—we have pants and jackets in the general human range, so you don't need to bring your own whites. And you'll just need a chef's knife, a utility and a paring knife. No need to bring your forty-pound kit tomorrow." He nodded without returning my gaze.

"Is there anything else you can think of?" I asked hopefully. He said only that he'd like to keep the menu if I didn't mind so that he could study it a bit before his trail. Done deal. We shook hands again, miraculously.

For the rest of the day I thought that maybe he wasn't blind, and that just because his eyes rolled around didn't mean he couldn't make out shape and color. But then I thought shape shmape and color shmolor, how is this guy going to dice a white onion on a white cutting board? I thought maybe I was an ignorant jerk who didn't realize how far the blind had come. Maybe he had worked out some kind of system to compensate. I took a mental inventory of famous accomplished blind people. Could playing the piano be anything like grilling fish over open flame, in the midst of hot fryer fat, sharp knives, macho line cooks and slippery floors? What was the preferred term for "blind" these days, anyway?

By the morning of his trail, I had talked myself into the certainty that though blind, he was obviously "sighted" in some other way. I felt sure that I was behind the times for thinking that just because someone was blind he couldn't work a job as a line cook in a busy restaurant. Or even be the lunch chef of one, as his résumé claimed. I knew, vaguely, that when a person lost one sense, the others kicked in expertly to compensate. I assured myself that he had developed a system by which he heard the food, or felt the food, or smelled which plate was used for which entrée. I became convinced that he, in fact, had evolved into such a higher species of line cook that we would learn greatness from him. I got so on board with the whole blind line cook thing that I was plainly righteous when asked by my incredulous and slightly unnerved line cooks why I had booked a trail with a blind guy. I practically had indignation in my tone. "What? You think just because the guy is 'visually challenged' that he can't cook in a restaurant?"

When he arrived for his trail I took him around on an introductory tour of the prep area and the walk-in and the hot line. At each station, he bent over and put his forehead against everything I showed him. It was fascinating at first—and later, heartbreaking—to note the angle at which he scrutinized each item in the refrigerator.

"Over here," I said, "is where all the proteins are kept. Fish here.
Meat here. Cooked above raw. Always. Okay?" And instead of
holding the pan of pork belly close under his nose and squinting
down upon it—like a very old man might do trying to read his
train ticket—he instead held each item up to his forehead, above
his eyebrows, and stared up imploringly into it.

We set him up in the basement prep area with a cutting board
and a menial task that wouldn't matter if he messed it up: picking
parsley. This took him most of the afternoon, and it was painful
to watch him bent in half, killing his back in order to have his
untethered eyes close up to the cutting board.

The trail is simply the time to sniff out the guy, to see how he
stands, how he holds his knives, how much he talks or doesn't and
what he says. Does he ravage everything with tongs or finesse with
a fork and a spoon? Does he sit at the bar at the end of his trail
and get hammered? Did he bring a pen and small pad of paper?
Did he thank the people who trailed him? I wasn't worried that
he was supposed to hold down the grill station. And I didn't give a
damn about the parsley. But I understood twenty-five minutes into
his trail that there was no system of compensation, that he had not
become hypersensate and that he had not, emphatically, evolved
into a superior cooking machine. Sadly, the guy was just plain
blind. And I still had on my hands another four hours thirty-five
minutes of a trail to honor.

The night started slowly, with just a couple of order tickets at a
time. I buckled myself into a seat at the back of the bus, so to speak,

right behind the blind guy in the grill station, and let my sous-chef do the driving: calling out the tickets and their timing, expediting their plating and pickups. Every time an order came into our station, I quietly narrated the procedure to the trailer, and watched, slack-jawed, as he painstakingly retrieved a portion of meat from the cooler, held it to his forehead, set it on a plate and then proceeded to carefully season the countertop with an even sprinkling of salt. When the call to "fire"—start cooking—an item came, I stood back and let him place the meat onto the grill—which he managed—but I had to pull him back a few inches from the flames so he wouldn't singe his bangs.

Eventually we fell into a kind of spontaneous, unfunny vaudeville routine in which I shadowed him, without his knowing, and seasoned the meat he missed, turned the fish he couldn't, moved the plate under his approaching spatula to receive the pork, like an outfielder judging a fly ball in Candlestick Park. I was not worried about him slowing down the line, as we never expect a trailer to actually perform a vital function. But I really started to feel sick with worry when he pulled a full fresh piping-hot basket of shoestring fries up out of the fat with his right hand and turned them out to drain—not into the waiting stack of giant coffee filters he held in his left hand, but into the thin air directly adjacent, pouring them out onto the dirty rubber mats and his clogs.

This did not escape the notice of the other cooks. All the light-heartedness of a good night on the line went right up the exhaust

hood. The banter between salad and sauté came to a screech-
ing halt. The fun part of getting through the night—donkey
noises, addressing the male line cooks as "ladies," as in, "Let's go,
ladies!"—was abandoned. The stern but softhearted barking from
the sous-chef down the line lost all playful bite and was tamed
down to the most perfunctory, gently articulated "Please fire apps
on seven." With one basket of hot fries cascading to the ground,
we all saw at once that this fellow was in physical danger.

In silence, I raked the fries up off the floor, trashed them and
dropped another order on the double. I asked him, kindly, to step
back to the wall and just watch a bit, explaining that the pace was
about to pick up and I wanted to keep the line moving. This is—
even when you have all your wits—the most humiliating part of a
trail: when the chef takes you off of the line in the middle of your
task. You die a thousand deaths. For a blind guy with something
to prove, maybe two thousand.

To this point I had somehow been willing to participate in whatever strange exercise this guy was putting himself through. I was
suspending disbelief, as we are all asked to do every time we go to a
play or a movie. I know that this isn't real, but I agree to believe that
it is for these two hours without intermission. But something about
the realization of the danger he was flirting with in service of his
project, whatever his project was, suddenly made me furious. I took
over the station and started slamming food onto the plates, narrat-
ing my actions to him in barely suppressed snide tones. "This," I

practically hissed, "is the pickup on the prawns. Three in a stack, napped with anchovy butter. Wanna write that down?"

I exhausted myself with passive-aggressive vitriol. "On the rack of lamb, you want an internal temp of one twenty-five. Just read the thermometer, okay?"

This got the attention of my sous-chef, who quietly came over and asked the guy if he'd like to step into garde-manger (the cold station) for a while to see how things there ran. I was relieved to have the guy away from the fire and the fat and in the relatively harmless oasis of cold leafy salads and cool creamy dressings. And I was grateful to be rescued from my worst self. The guy spent the rest of his trail with his back up against the wall in all the stations, eyes rolling around in his head, pretending to apprehend how each station worked. I spent the remainder of his trail wrestling meat and unattractive feelings triggered by this insane predicament in which we had found ourselves.

I never did find out what he was doing. I allowed him to finish out the whole trail, and when he had changed his clothes, I encouraged him to sit at the bar and have something to eat, which he did. And as he was leaving, I said I would call him the next day, which I did. I told him that I was looking for someone with a little more power, a bit more of a heavy hitter, but that I would keep him in mind if a position more aligned with his skills became available.

This, remarkably, he seemed to see coming.

Loss

Expatriate Games

JOHN BURNHAM SCHWARTZ

John Burnham Schwartz is the author of four novels, including
The Commoner *and* Reservation Road, *which was made into
a feature film based on his screenplay.*

W hen I moved to Paris in 1989 to work on a second
novel, I hadn't seen Alex in twenty years. We played
together as kids, then fell out of touch. By the time
we became reacquainted in Paris, I barely recognized him. He had
thick, ink black, curly hair, ringlets almost, that seemed to shine
with some secretly applied ointment, and he wore a hat, a cool,
slightly insouciant number, part Belmondo and part Boyer, that
went nicely with his patterned waistcoats and the long key chain
that looped out of his pants pocket and the hand-rolled cigarettes
he smoked day and night.

He had come to Paris to study at the Ritz cooking school, then landed an apprenticeship at Taillevent, one of the world's most celebrated restaurants. Yet in no time, fed up with chopping onions ten hours a day, he quit Taillevent. Quit Taillevent! But that was to be expected. It was the feeding of friends he believed in; in his mind, chopping onions for strangers was an entirely different, somehow smaller-hearted enterprise. He cooked the way he ate, and he ate like Orson Welles or Brando in their later, Roman-emperor days—as if he were going to swallow the world, but all in his own good time.

I introduced him to my circle of twenty-something American friends: Deb, a photojournalist; Josh, a television executive; Olivia, a philosopher; Phyllida, an editor; Lucy, a playwright. Most of us had gone to college together but had made our way to Paris for our own reasons, which, as with young people everywhere, had to do mostly with longing and possibility, a kind of permanent hunger. We wanted to step outside our normal lives and rebuild a community from scratch. We did this by spending a lot of time together, and by eating and drinking as much as possible. This, of course, was the sort of mission Alex was born to join. No one in my gang had ever met anyone quite like him. He said that he cooked, and we thought, Oh, he cooks, but we didn't know what that meant until the night he invited all of us for dinner.

He was renting a drafty artist's studio off the Rue du Temple. The kitchen was primitive, just two electric burners and an old toaster oven. None of the dining chairs matched. The silverware had been stolen from various cafés, and the glasses were shirt-cleaned.

That night Alex cracked open fat cloves of garlic with the side of a chef's knife and rubbed them, with the best virgin olive oil, over thick slices of peasant bread, then toasted them lightly in the toaster oven. Next he served us a slow-cooked Bolognese sauce of such earthy sweetness and meaty depth that it seemed at once ancient and new. To this day, the memory of its taste is wedded in my mind to the cymbal-like crash of Alex banging pots in the kitchen.

From that night onward, Sunday dinner at Alex's became our weekly ritual. Between feasts—and sometimes during—life-altering decisions were made, hearts broken, songs badly sung. People came and went. For a few uncomfortable months, Josh the TV executive and I shared a girlfriend. Lucy the playwright arrived in the City of Light with an arrogant, pasty-faced, vegan boyfriend none of us liked, but then one Sunday she showed up at dinner on the back of a Frenchman's motorcycle, suffused with an unmistakable glow. Overnight she had become, as it were, a carnivore, and we responded by toasting her liberation and welcoming Yves into the gang. Ditto for Paul, the huge-hearted Russian who stole Deb the photojournalist's heart one night at a party; the following Sunday he became one of us, and is still.

And so it went. Sunday morning would roll around, and each

of us would receive a mumbled phone call from a very hungover Alex: You, bring bread! You, haricots verts! You, wine! You, fresh sage! The meal's centerpiece—the lamb shoulder, the Cornish hens, the poulet de Bresse—our chef would trust to no one but himself. Dressed like a dandified gangster, he would roam the narrow streets around the Rue du Temple and in his highly eccentric French discuss the freshly killed birds with the butcher.

That evening we would arrive on his doorstep with our packages and find him already on his third glass of Bordeaux and his umpteenth cigarette. An apron, folded in half and tied at his waist, a dish towel draped over his left shoulder: the calm before the storm.

He always started slowly. But as the group arrived and the room grew lively with voices in French and English, Alex's spirits seemed to rise commensurately with the delicious odors. By ten o'clock we would be salivating like animals and he would just be warming up. He was one of those insane people, a renegade magician, insufferable to live with but impossible to look away from, who could spin culinary gold out of the dross of a few dried herbs and a handful of grain. It was like being in an artist's studio as he painted—face to face with the creative moment, the choices made on the spot, the diving forward. He finished Cornish game hens in the toaster oven, using a sable-hair paintbrush to glaze them. On Thanksgiving, he peeled back the skin of a turkey, stuffed it with truffles, then sewed it back together again. He sautéed brussels sprouts with cubes of pancetta and stood poached pears upright in a frangipane tart dusted with crushed almonds.

Thinking about him now, I'm struck by what seems an obvious thought: that it was not the backbreaking toil that Alex hated in restaurant jobs, or even the submission to the necessities of commerce, but the insulation of the closed kitchen door. Who wants to be a madman locked away in a closet? For our part, we were as much alarmed by him as we were enthralled by the tastes he introduced us to.

Then, all too soon, it was over. Deb and Paul left for Moscow, Josh for Madrid, Lucy and Phyllida and I for America. Alex wrapped up his chef's knives and went home, too. I had dinner with him in New York a couple of times, but somehow, after Paris, any other city was an uneasy fit. I remember him coming to my apartment one night and emptying my vodka supply and dropping burning cigarette ash on my rug and inadvertently breaking a chair—but also, of course, roasting the best capon I have ever eaten in my life.

Sixteen years later, our old Paris group remains in close touch. Everyone except Alex, that is. The rumor is that he's on the West Coast making priceless objets d'art out of bronze. We talk about him the way you talk about a bungee jump once made from a very high, very beautiful cliff: How vivid the colors were! How alive we felt! How pathetically safe not to have him now in our mature, ordered lives! Yet one day without warning—I simply feel it—he will come back to us, his knives sharp as ever, his pots and pans filled with music.

FRANGIPANE PEAR TART

FOR THE PEARS

2 cups sugar

3 strips lemon peel

9 firm-ripe small pears, such as Seckel

1. Combine the sugar, lemon peel and 8 cups water in a large saucepan. Bring to a boil over high heat, stirring to dissolve the sugar. Turn off the heat and set aside to cool.
2. When the liquid is cool enough to touch, begin preparing the pears. Using a small melon baller or a small curved knife and starting from the core end, carefully scoop a tunnel through the center of one of the pears, removing all of the seeds while keeping the pear whole. Peel the pear, leaving the stem intact, and immediately add it to the cooking liquid so that it doesn't brown. Repeat with the rest of the pears.
3. Turn the heat to high under the pears and return the liquid to a boil. Lower the heat so that the pears are barely simmering and cook just until the pears feel barely tender when pierced with a sharp knife, about 5 minutes. Remove from the heat and cool the pears in the cooking liquid.

FOR THE PASTRY

9 tablespoons unsalted butter, at room temperature

3 1/2 tablespoons superfine sugar

1 large egg, lightly beaten

1/8 teaspoon vanilla extract

Pinch salt

1 3/4 cups flour

1. Fit a mixer with the paddle attachment. Over medium speed, cream the butter and sugar until very light. Combine the egg, vanilla and salt and with the mixer running, gradually add the egg (about a teaspoon at a time), scraping down the sides of the bowl with a rubber spatula once or twice. Add the flour in three parts and continue to mix just until you have a soft, uniform dough. Form the dough into a ball and then flatten into a disc, wrap in plastic and refrigerate for at least 30 minutes and up to 3 days.

2. Let the dough rest at room temperature for about 5 minutes before rolling it out. On a lightly floured surface, roll the dough into a circle about a 1/8-inch thick and use it to line a 9-inch tart pan with a removable bottom. Return to the refrigerator for 20 minutes and preheat the oven to 350 degrees. Line the tart pan with parchment paper, fill with pie weights and chill for another 5 minutes.

3. Bake for 15 minutes, carefully remove the parchment and weights, and bake for another 5 minutes or so, until the bot-

tom of the crust looks dry and the edges are lightly browned. Set aside to cool on a rack while you make the frangipane, leaving the oven on.

FOR THE FRANGIPANE

7 tablespoons unsalted butter, at room temperature
1 cup ground almonds
2 large eggs
2 tablespoons flour
7 tablespoons superfine sugar
Pinch salt

In the bowl of a mixer fitted with a paddle attachment, cream the butter over medium speed until light. Add the almonds and blend well. Add one of the eggs and the flour, mixing until combined. Scrape down the sides of the bowl with a spatula, add the second egg, the sugar and the salt, and mix just until smooth. Set aside until ready to use.

FOR THE ASSEMBLY

3 tablespoons apricot jam
2 tablespoons toasted slivered almonds, lightly crushed

1. To assemble the tart, drain the poached pears upright on a towel for a few minutes. Spread the frangipane evenly into the tart shell and place one pear, stem-end up, in the center of the tart,

gently pushing it down into the frangipane. Arrange 6 more pears in a circle around the first pear, choosing the best-looking pears (you will have 2 left over). Bake for about 30 minutes, until the frangipane is evenly browned and set.

2. Heat the apricot jam with 1 tablespoon of water in a small saucepan and lightly brush the pears with this glaze. Sprinkle the crushed almonds evenly over the top of the tart. Cool and serve at room temperature.

Serves 8 to 10

Inward Bound

CHANG-RAE LEE

Chang-rae Lee is the author of three novels and teaches fiction writing at Princeton University.

At the lowest point of my life, I was cooking all the time. Normally, I cook most when I'm feeling contented, say, when the writing is going decently well and the family is happy. But during the fall of 1990, I was cooking and miserable.

I was twenty-five years old, sharing an apartment in Manhattan; two years earlier I had quit a first job on Wall Street to try to become a novelist, and had a lot of nothing to show for it, 500 pages of a book that was terribly clever and impressive but compelled no one. I had run through my savings and was guiltily living on the largesse of my parents, who were paying the whole of the mortgage and maintenance on the co-op we had originally purchased "together" when I signed on for the fancy position.

For food and drink while I was writing the Great Novel, I took on occasional jobs, writing articles for a free downtown newspaper, temping as a secretary for the dean at a fashion school, playing production assistant on modeling shoots. I couldn't afford taking dates out to restaurants, so I made precious, odd-ingredient dinners, overplaying my hand as the struggling but resourceful artist. But on top of all that—which by most lights should only be a welcome period of youthful, romantic folly and self-inflicted toil—my mother was enduring stomach cancer.

The one good thing was that I was able to go up to Syracuse to see her whenever I wanted, or was needed; mostly what I'd do was take care of the house, the cleaning and cooking. "You should be at your desk, not in the kitchen," my mother would say, but I knew better; not writing was a relief. I'd prepare the Korean dishes she always made, the scallion pancakes and clam-and-spinach soup and broiled porgies and an assortment of banchan—side dishes of vegetables and savories.

I was cooking well, strangely well, though the better a dish turned out, the more somber our mood grew. My mother was no longer really eating then. But what else was there to do? I was cooking for my father, who came home each night with fresh hope on his face that would soon give way to an epochal weariness, and for myself, to keep moving as much as I could and to feed my own brutally keen hunger. And I think now that I was cooking most of all for my mother, who would take a scant taste of my offerings, for a salve, for a memory.

When I'd return to New York, a hollowed-out feeling would bloom in my gut. I was working like a fiend, trying to chip away at the homely rock of my novel but succeeding only in making it smaller and more misshapen than it already was. The only solace of the day was to make food—the basic things, soups, simple pastas and bread.

I'd get up and start the yeast and then sit down to my work and then take breaks to punch down the rising dough. By midday there would be some passable baguettes that my roommate and I would eat with apple butter, and later, after I finally depleted myself with the writing, I'd wander down First Avenue and try to buy dinner provisions for less than ten dollars, including a very cheap bottle of wine, some tawny vin de pays from the closeout bin, the dregs of which I'd use for an ersatz puttanesca sauce the next day, substituting green olives for the capers, which seemed, like everything else in my life, much too dear.

Those days ran into one another, the dreary rhythm broken only by a call one evening: my father saying in a lean, quiet voice that perhaps now was a good time to return home. I was just finishing the last revisions on the novel, so I planned to print out the book, send it off to an editor and take the train upstate. Printing hundreds of pages took a long time with a daisy-wheel printer, literally half a day, and I passed the time by renting a few movies I wanted to see, *Tampopo* and *Babette's Feast*. *Tampopo*, of course, is the great Japanese noodle-soup western, hilarious and delectable and full of a certain sorrowful beauty for the pleasures of eating, but it was *Babette's Feast* that stopped my heart.

The film is about a Parisian chef named Babette who escapes the Communard uprising of 1871 and lives for fourteen years in the harsh Jutland region of Denmark, where she has been given refuge by a pair of kind spinsters who head a religious sect in their bleak seaside village. The sisters, we learn, have sacrificed their early talents and hopes—one for singing, the other a true love—for the sake of sustaining their father's sect. Babette submerges her culinary talents—she is one of the great chefs of Paris—while living with them, contenting herself with cooking endless piles of fish.

But when she hits the lottery, she decides to repay their kindness with a seven-course meal for the sect members, who giddily delight in the exquisite richness of the caille en sarcophage and baba au rhum, and even ask for second glasses of the "lemonade," which is in fact Champagne. The lifeblood rises in their faces and, we think, in their hearts too. When the sisters realize that Babette has spent all her money on this one meal, they ask her how she will possibly get by now, how she will ever be able to return someday to Paris. Babette answers that she will manage, and utters, with a solemn resolve, "An artist is never poor."

I broke down at that moment, the only time I've cried because of a movie, the tears and sobs coming so hard that finally I had to use the sofa pillow to quell myself. And although I would relinquish most everything to report that it went well afterward, that I returned home and my mother miraculously recovered and is still savoring the days, I cannot. It would prove to be her last season, her last Thanksgiving and Christmas. That novel was gently but firmly rejected. It is in most every measure gone. And yet, what remains is the notion—no, the insistence—that overwhelmed me then: one ought never give up. Never. Even when you've lost all.

Our Lady of Lawson

PICO IYER

Pico Iyer is the author of seven works of nonfiction, including
The Lady and the Monk, The Global Soul *and, most recently,*
The Open Road, *and of two novels.*

To live in Japan without eating Japanese food seems an advanced kind of heresy. My sushi-loving friends in California regard me as a lost cause; my housemates in Japan simply shrug and see this as ultimate confirmation—me dragging at some lasagna in a plastic box while they gobble down dried fish—that I belong to an alien species. I grew up in England, I tell them, on boarding school food, no less; I like Japan at some level deeper than the visible (or edible). They look away and try not to scream.

Yet the habit that has won me complete excommunication on both sides of the world is my readiness to eat (twice a day) from Lawson, my tiny local convenience store in Nara, the old Japanese capital. A convenience store speaks to many of us of all that is questionable in modern Japan: a soulless, synthetic, one-size-fits-all lifestyle that the efficiency-loving country has perfected to the nth degree. It marks, most would say, the end of family, tradition and community as well as the advent of a homogenized future that has many people running for "slow food."

The convenience store is a model of Japan in miniature: the triumph of function over fuss and of ease over embarrassment. Just as you can buy whiskey, eggs, pornography and even (it is said) women's underwear in vending machines, so you can all but live in convenience stores. I pay my phone bills and send my packages through the local branch of the national Lawson chain (named after the defunct American Lawson); I buy my bus cards there and tickets for Neil Young concerts. I make the convenience store my de facto office, lingering by the photocopier for hours on end and then faxing an article, say, to New York. Yet the first law of Japan, even in Lawson, is that nothing is what it seems, and that you can find all the cultures of the world here, made Japanese and strange. Here, in the four thin aisles of my local store, are the McVitie's digestives of my youth—turned into bite-size afterthoughts. Here are Milky Bar chocolates, converted into bullet-size pellets. Here are Mentos in shades of lime and grape, cans of "Strawberry Milk

Tea" and the Smarties I used to collect as a boy, refashioned as "Marble Chocolate." Were Marcel Proust to come to Lawson, he would find his madeleines daily but made smaller, sweeter and mnemonically new.

It's common to hear that Japan has created a promiscuous anthology of the world's best styles. And the convenience store is the center of this. Tubs of Earl Grey ice cream, sticks of mangosteen chewing gum, green-tea-flavored Kit Kat bars: they're all here in abundance (though, in fashion-victimized Japan, no sooner have I developed a fondness for KissMint chewing gum "for Etiquette" than it has been supplanted by ice creams in the shape of watermelon slices). And even the smallest chocolate bar comes with an English-language inscription that, in the Japanese way, makes no sense whatsoever, yet confers on everything the perfume of an enigmatic fairy tale: "A lovely and tiny twig," says my box of Koeda chocolates, "is a heroine's treasured chocolate born in the forest."

In modern Japan, the convenience store is taken to be the spiritual home of the boys in hip-hop shorts and the girls with shocking yellow hair and artificial tans, who try with their every move—eating in the street, squatting on the sidewalk—to show that they take their cues from 50 Cent and not Mrs. Suzuki. The door of my local Lawson has badges to denote police surveillance, and where the great twentieth-century novelist Junichiro Tanizaki praised shadows (nuance, ambiguity, the lure of the half-seen) as the essence of the Japan he loved, Lawson speaks for a new fluorescent, posthuman—even anti-Japanese—future. And yet, in the twelve years I've lived on and off in my mock-California suburb, the one person who has come to embody for me all the care for detail and solicitude I love in Japan is, in fact, the lady at the cash register in Lawson. Small, short-haired and perpetually harried, Hirata-san races to the back of the store to fetch coupons for me that will give me ten cents off my "Moisture Dessert." She bows to the local gangster who leaves his Bentley running and comes in the store with his high-heeled moll to claim some litchi-flavored strangeness. When occasionally I don't show up for six or seven hours, she sends, through my housemates, a bag of French fries to revive me.

The Japanese are so good at keeping up appearances that few signs are ever evident of the series of recent recessions. But over the years, I have seen poor Mrs. Hirata's husband (the store's manager) open his doors around the clock and take the graveyard shift himself. The place started to stock tequila-sunrise cocktails in a can, and little bottles of wine. Soon even the Hiratas' two high-school-age sons were being pressed into service (unpaid, I'm sure).

It's no easier to understand Japan in Western terms than it is to eat noodles with a knife and fork. Yet it has been evident to me for some time that the crush of the anonymous world lies out in the temple-filled streets; the heart of the familiarity, the communal sense of neighborhood, the simple kindness that brought me to Japan, lies in the convenience store.

Early last year, writing an article on paradise, I surmised that my modest neighborhood could be improved only by the addition of a cinema, but given the laws of human longing and limitation, such an arrival would probably mean the end of my favorite convenience store. Be careful of what you write. Days before my article came out, a sign appeared on my local Lawson, announcing it was going out of business. Almost everyone in the neighborhood was shaken, but no one knew what to do. (How to express your gratitude to a convenience store?) We'd watched the owners' sons grow up while their parents served up bags of chicken nuggets in three spicy flavors.

I went home, found a set of elegant bowls I'd bought in case of a sudden need for a wedding present, and returned to the store. They were being transferred to a far-off shop in the countryside, Mrs. Hirata said; she feared for her kids. She was even afraid of going out there herself. Then I handed over the box, and she realized why I had come. She began to waver for a moment, then turned away from me and put a calzone in the microwave. A true Japanese to the end, she wanted to protect me from her tears.

American Dreams

Jon Robin Baitz is the author of several plays, including The
Substance of Fire, A Fair Country, The Paris Letter, The
Film Society *and* Three Hotels. *He is the creator and executive
producer of the ABC TV drama* Brothers & Sisters.

When I was a teenager in the 1970s, I lived with my
parents in Durban, South Africa, where my father
had been sent by his employer, Carnation Milk. It
was here that I learned about homesickness and the odd melancho-
lia of Sundays in foreign places. When we arrived from Los Angeles
in 1972, I was a wary ten-year-old, and my impressions of the place
were formed as I got off the plane and saw the "This Door for
Whites Only" sign in the terminal. Over the next few years, I came
to recognize the colonial old-boy British superiority for what it
was: a poison toad, the last gasps of a dying empire, only surpassed

in its lazy smugness by the breathtaking meanness of the Afrikaners and their ruling Nationalist Party. I was very lonely.

By the time I was thirteen, the stories of the American civil rights movement and the Underground Railroad were both my holy scripture and my Batman comics. But my patriotism, like a lot of patriotism, was actually a brand of nostalgia, which was, at its core, culinary and sensual as much as it was idealistic. What I really missed was the easy playfulness of my life in Southern California and its talismanic seventies coolness: Jackson Browne, the Eagles, 7-Elevens, corduroys from the Gap and the casual vernacular of L.A.'s food—double cheeseburgers from Fat Burger, chili dogs from Pink's on La Brea or tacos from El Coyote (places around the corner from our old Spanish colonial house). None of it was good, but all of it was perfect. Because to me, it was the food of my lost pop life, one that had nothing to do with complicity and apartheid, one that rejected the dull mushy-peas probity of Durban's white cuisine. No. The food I ate in Durban, prepared by servants trained by generations of Anglo-African hausfraus, was not the cuisine of democracy, so I dreamed of L.A.'s drive-throughs. Of going to the car wash with my dad and eating taquitos by the stand in the parking lot as his old Fairlane was being washed. How could a cool iceberg salad with Russian dressing served by an elderly waitress at the late, lamented Dolores's Drive In on Wilshire Boulevard seem like a perfect refutation of apartheid? Easy. Because at Dolores's, you didn't have to be white like me in order to get fries and a Coke.

At school, in my *Lord of the Flies* uniform, lunch was greasy shepherd's pies and Cornish pasties, scarfed down next to boys who would cheerfully remind me that there would soon come a day when the violence would begin in earnest. Looking out at the Indian Ocean, they would parrot the predictive mantras of their parents; of killings in the streets and oncoming armies of black servants turning on us without mercy and without relent. These whispered predictions (along with advice on the prudence of becoming proficient in the language of the pistol and the shotgun) were chapter and verse of white South African life then. But it was only on Sundays that the fear got to me. Then Durban would simply shut itself down. It was in this earsplitting silence that white Durban and its churchy rectitude became almost hallucinatory. Aside from the scurrying feet of geckos and the buzz of mosquitoes and the barking dogs, often the only noise came from radios in other houses, emanating hymns or Afrikaner folk music. On Sundays, Durban entirely rejected sensation. No movies. No television. Both were an affront to God at the time. (His will changed later.) Only silence. And on those Sundays, with aunts and uncles and cousins and old friends thousands of miles away, I realized how much I missed simply fitting in. A Sunday dinner with people you've known forever, replete with bickering, gossip and asides. Even the dull silence of a happy family. Anything but Durban's silence.

We ended up finding a decrepit country club where my dad sometimes played golf, and to my joy, movies would be shown, projected onto a sheet from a shaky 16-millimeter projector. There was no consistency: bad American movies of the 1970s; odd Ealing comedies of the 1950s; late-era John Wayne, when he tried to be a detective; spaghetti westerns; or occasional gems like *The Last of Sheila* and *Wait Until Dark*, where someone leaps out of the blackness at a blind Audrey Hepburn. Or three episodes in a row of *The Mod Squad*, during which the clubhouse would go silent while the drunken Durbanites hypnotically watched the screen while black people did cool things or struck whitey.

Between reels, dinner would be served, and there I found the corollary to my missed L.A. street food in the vivid, angry, gloriously hot red curries prepared by Indian cooks, descendants of indentured Indian servants who arrived in Durban on tramp steamers in 1860 to work in the sugar plantations north of the city. The film would stop at some almost arbitrary moment in the plot, as a reel ran out, and people would wander up to a steam table and fill their plates. Steve McQueen could wait. You could never forget where you were: at a broken-down country club on a golf course at the edge of the Indian Ocean, a golf course where monkeys habitually shot out of the trees to swipe balls and run screaming back into the jungle. One night, the club screened Norman Jewison's *In the Heat of the Night*, starring Sidney Poitier as a smart cop working a murder case in the deep American South, gradually winning over the white sheriff played by Rod Steiger. Poitier shamed and made fools of the denizens of the town, who basically seemed like your average white Durbanite. At the end of the second reel, one of the locals turned to me and said, "Our kaffirs aren't smart like your American niggers." I sneered at him, and there was a moment—and then he went off to drink some beer with several rattled friends. I stuck to myself.

Durban curry is famously spicy, and that heat was a perfect antidote to the becalmed Durban Sundays. There was sweat, and there was pain, but that was made even more exciting when it was washed down with icy local beer. The scent of lamb and potatoes simmering in a masala of cardamom, cinnamon, cloves and coriander mingled with the sweet darkness of the chilies, and the tartness of tomatoes was a tonic. This was a food of the people, something actual, real, as much as it was delicious and complicated. After the long dinner breaks, the projector would be turned on again. By then, it would be late, and most of the audience would be drunk. You could barely see the screen through the cigarette smoke, and the hecklers would have quieted. And in those moments, in the dark, watching some movie, I would be reminded that there were things to look forward to, there were chapters to come.

DURBAN LAMB CURRY WITH TOMATO
AND MINT SAMBAL

FOR THE TOMATO AND MINT SAMBAL
2 ripe tomatoes, diced

4 mint leaves, finely chopped

1 green chili, finely diced

2 teaspoons red wine vinegar

Pinch of sugar

FOR THE LAMB CURRY

2 tablespoons canola or vegetable oil

1 large onion, sliced into rings

1 sprig curry leaves

2 garlic cloves, finely chopped

1 teaspoon grated ginger

3 teaspoons curry masala

1 teaspoon ground cumin

1 teaspoon ground coriander

1 teaspoon ground cinnamon

1/2 teaspoon ground turmeric

1/2 teaspoon ground cardamom

1/4 teaspoon ground cloves

2 pounds boneless leg of lamb, cut into 1-inch cubes

3 small dried red chilies, left whole

Salt

2 medium tomatoes, cored and diced

7 ounces chicken broth

1 teaspoon tomato paste

4 medium white potatoes, peeled and diced

Fresh coriander leaves, to serve

1. Make the tomato and mint sambal first: Mix all the ingredients together, cover and chill for an hour before serving.

2. For the lamb curry: Heat the oil in a large frying pan and cook the onion and curry leaves until the onion is soft and golden brown. Stir in the garlic, ginger and spices and cook for a couple of minutes over a low heat.

3. Increase the temperature and add the lamb and chilies, browning the lamb, and stirring occasionally for 3 to 5 minutes. Season with salt.

4. Add the tomatoes, half the broth, and cook for about 10 minutes; then add the tomato paste.

5. Add the potatoes and the remaining broth; cover and simmer until the lamb and potatoes are tender, about 15 minutes.

6. Remove the chilies and curry leaves, adjust the seasoning, and sprinkle with the coriander before serving. Serve with the tomato and mint sambal.

Serves 4

Adapted from Alan Coxon, a host of *Great Food Live* on UKTV.

Compliments of the Nurse

DAWN DRZAL

Dawn Drzal writes about food, travel and fiction for the New York Times *and other publications. Her essay "Guilty" appeared in the collection* Mommy Wars.

The unevenly typed postcard in my shaking hand is from M.F.K. Fisher. It's the spring of 1987, I'm twenty-six years old and to me she's more than the doyenne of food writers: she's a goddess, a combination of Colette and Julia Child. I had written several weeks before, asking to interview her for a book I hope to write about her and her work. "Come for lunch," the postcard says.

Lunch is in Glen Ellen, California—three thousand miles away from my apartment in Cambridge, Massachusetts—so it is June before my rental car clanks over the cattle guards to the Bouverie Ranch. "Trespassers Will Be Violated" reads a sign tacked to a tree. The small white stucco house is artfully concealed between two hills. Now that my dearest wish is about to be granted, I am sick with dread. Only the knowledge that I would never forgive myself keeps me from turning the car around.

On the phone the night before, M.F.K. Fisher insisted I call her Mary Frances and said she was recovering from a bad fall.

"But arrive as early as you like, dear. If I'm asleep, you just come in."

"It'll be like the *levée*," I said, referring to Louis XIV's ritual of waking to a roomful of courtiers.

She laughed ruefully. "Not exactly."

I swallow hard and call her name through the half-open door. No answer. When I step inside, I am startled to find her regarding me with a keen blue-gray gaze from a desk heaped with papers.

"I answered you, dear," her voice is faint and quavery, "but you didn't hear me." She holds out her hand. "You look very nice."

"So do you," I say.

She is still beautiful at seventy-eight: freshly made up, with high cheekbones and a mouth, familiar from a hundred photographs, that manages to be both sensual and somewhat peevish. She is, in fact, just as I had imagined her—until she stands up. Then the toll of Parkinson's, arthritis and a recent hip implant become apparent. What she most fiercely resents is that they have left her unable to live alone. She tells me that I have been asked to lunch so early this Saturday because her live-in companion is singing at a Golden Gate Bridge fiftieth-anniversary celebration.

As she makes her way to the kitchen, which stretches along the far wall, I have time to look around. It seems impossible that this expanse of living room, with its domed redwood ceiling and glossy black-tile floor, open on all sides to pastures and distant mountains, could have been hidden behind the façade of a modest ranch house. There are books everywhere—not just the famous cookbook collection near the kitchen, but ordinary and rare editions spilling out of built-in bookcases, piled on tables, stacked on the floor. Later I hope to have a look at some of them, and to settle for myself whether a Picasso or a Matisse hangs in the red-lacquer bathroom.

"I was up until five," she is saying as she lowers herself into a chair by the kitchen table. "Then this morning I lay listening to the comedy hour on the radio, dozing and chuckling."

"Are you an insomniac?" I venture.

"Oh, I don't know about that, dear. Insomniacs mind, don't they?"

Under her instructions, I assemble our lunch on the shady, colonnaded porch overlooking a meadow. To my joy, she asks me to set the table with the chipped green plates from Provence I have eaten from so often in my imagination, the Mexican goblets, a few cheeses selected from the steady stream provided by local friends and visitors hoping to please, a bottle of Glen Ellen Chardonnay (left, surprisingly, uncorked overnight in the refrigerator), a loaf of rock-hard bread, a sweet tiny cantaloupe and slices of a ham someone smoked for her.

When everything is on the table, she asks me to pour her a drink—equal parts gin, dry vermouth and Campari in a large, squat tumbler. No ice. She sips at it through lunch, which she barely touches.

"I really don't like to eat very much," she says after asking me to bring out some rice pudding for dessert. "The only reason I eat is because of the pills."

I shouldn't be surprised, given her age, but I feel as if the pope had just leaned over and confided that he says Mass these days only because the faithful expect it. To hide my discomfiture, I ask if I can set up my tape recorder and ask her a few questions. She agrees, and when I get settled, she smiles mischievously. "Now, you ask me something really profound, and I will give you the answer."

I laugh nervously. "Well, um, I wanted to ask you about food, but just because—"

"About my first meal . . . my mother's breast."

"Okay, let me ask you something not about food—"

To my relief, the front door bangs. Mary Frances raises her eyebrows and leans over conspiratorially. "Now, you mustn't mind Mary Jane. She thinks visitors exhaust me." A tiny but powerfully built woman appears with a handful of pills and a glass of water. The look she gives me tells me my time is up.

"Where's your costume?" Mary Frances asks solicitously. "Didn't you dress up as the Statue of Liberty?"

"I took it off." She slides the glass closer to Mary Frances. "Here—a friendly reminder."

"Pills, pills, pills," Mary Frances says in a singsong voice.

"Pills, pills, pills, pills, pills," Mary Jane echoes, not to be outdone.

"Aren't you nasty," Mary Frances says.

"You're nasty," Mary Jane parrots. She reappears on the porch a moment later with her hands cupped in front of her. "I've got something to show you," she says, her voice rising portentously, "if it won't make you sick."

"Nothing makes me sick," Mary Frances retorts.

Mary Jane opens her hands to reveal a trembling field mouse, its front paws pressed together as if in supplication.

"Poor little thing. Just toss him over the railing."

"No. I'm not going to toss him quite like that. He's a sweetheart."

"What are you going to do with him?" Mary Frances calls out after her. "I'll bet you eat that little mouse."

In the airport that night, I decide to check to see what was captured on the tape in my cassette player, which I had left running after our interview session was cut short. Rummaging in the bottom of my backpack, my fingers travel over something unexpectedly stiff and furry. I pull my hand out as if it were on fire. The walls of the waiting room begin to melt and shimmer. If I don't instantly plunge my hand in again, I know I will never be able to do it—not to get my airline ticket, the tape, my wallet. So I wrap a paper napkin around my hand, close my eyes and manage to grab the tail. With a sickening lurch, I toss the little corpse into a metal ashtray and cover it with the napkin.

I don't know how long I sit there asking myself what on earth could possess a person to do such a thing before I remember the end of the afternoon. Embarrassed to knock again after my rushed goodbye, I had slipped back into the house to use the bathroom (where, to the right of the sink, hung a Picasso drawing, not a Matisse). Unobserved, I had watched Mary Jane walk Mary Frances down the hall to the bedroom, supporting her around the waist with a sturdy arm. Reaching the doorway, Mary Frances sagged with such palpable relief against the younger woman's body that I was pierced with the awareness that Mary Frances simply couldn't afford to resent the person upon whom she depended so completely. I, not Mary Jane, was the interloper. That mouse was simply the messenger.

Coming Home

Turning Japanese

HEIDI JULAVITS

Heidi Julavits is a founding editor of The Believer, *a monthly books and culture magazine. Her most recent novel is* The Uses of Enchantment.

I graduated from college in 1990, an uncertain time indeed. Recession. Gulf war imminent. In keeping with the shaky global mood, I haven't a clue what to do with my life. So I decide to move to Japan to teach the only thing I can confidently claim to know after four years of college: English. In America, I reason, the only thing more shameful than not knowing what you want is knowing, with absolute certainty, that stuffed animals turn you on. In Japan I'll be immersed in a culture that nurtures uncertainty as a form of enlightenment. I remind myself of the

Zen-like quotation: "Emotional freedom comes with being aware of the certainty of uncertainty." I will go to Japan, I will be certainly uncertain and I will reach a higher plane of existence while eating amazing food.

I find a sublet in a functional-blah apartment building off Shijo Street in Kyoto, and two things happen: I remain unenlightened by my uncertainty, and I eat amazing food. A typical on-the-cheap lunch bowl, offered in local spots displaying dusty plastic food in the window, is katsu-don, a fried pork cutlet with scrambled eggs, served with rice and a sweet donburi sauce; or tekka-don, strips of raw tuna and pressed dried seaweed over rice. A Japanese family invites me to dinner each week for shabu shabu: a pot of water and enoki mushrooms, set on an electric tabletop coil, in which we poach very thin slices of beef or hacked-up Alaskan king crab; after the meat is finished, we dump our rice into the broth and slurp the resulting porridgy soup.

As the months pass, I remain miserably uncertain about all things but one: I would kill for a trashy American sweet. I do not miss cheese or pasta or even my friends, but I do miss, with a maddening intensity, that blast of sugar that only a glazed cruller can provide. Plenty of Japanese bakeries offer deceptively Western-looking cakes and cookies, which reveal themselves to be gaggingly dry and possessing a slight aftertaste of fish, as if whatever fat the baker used came not from a cow or a pig but from a hake. I patronize a previously disdained restaurant called Spaghetti and Cake

(Kyoto has a number of these "Western" establishments; another is Coffee and Golf) and am disappointed—huge shock. The best of the lousy bunch is ring cake, a rolled-up yellow sponge cut into slices. But one day while working as a movie extra in a period film (1850s Yokohama being the period), I am forced to wear a bonnet and eat slice after slice of ring cake because the lead, a Japanese pop star, can't remember her three short lines. I come to hate ring cake. When another American tells me about a Western breakfast restaurant, I bike ten miles through a downpour and order French toast as an excuse to deluge my plate with dyed-brown corn syrup, which I eat until I am headachingly ill.

I orchestrate my own intervention. I remind myself that everybody knows that ersatz American food, or ersatz any food, is a doomed proposition. You must play to a culture's strengths and not order a cataplana of paella when in Green Bay, Wisconsin. Yet my first encounters with the native sweets are alienating. Gummy lime green bean blobs dusted in a flavorless white flour, for example, are not only not sweet, but they also do not appeal to any of my tongue's five regions and are all the more disappointing for appearing so pretty.

One dusky evening I am biking through Gion, Kyoto's geisha district, examining the window displays with their meticulously wrapped I-don't-know-what. (Jewelry? Art supplies? Stew meat?) One helpfully exhibits what's concealed beneath the wrapping: a bloated Fig Newton look-alike bisected to reveal a dense and grainy maroon center. I buy what I learn, decades later, is called manju. The filling is a paste made from red azuki beans and sugar. I call it a bean cake. I bike to Gion every day and buy two.

And so it is that I come to grapple with that oldest of Zen mysteries: the bean-cake conundrum. Of course I've been paddling around this riddle for months, but it's not until I encounter the bean cake that it assumes its most potent form. While eating a bean cake, I reach a moment when I don't need, or want, another bite. I experience what I believe is contentment (rather than "no thought," think "no appetite"), and despite what my layman's notion of Zen Buddhist nongoal goals lead me to expect, it is no blissfest. My American relationship to sugar is always to want more of it; to encounter a sweet that doesn't court abuse in order to be enjoyed destabilizes my entire concept of craving-cruller-gluttony-happiness. I feel these moments of so-called contentment when I have no pointed desires—not a petit four to follow the chocolates to follow the tarte Tatin, not even a salt-funky cheese course as counterbalance—to be physically unbearable and thus, by quick extrapolation, existentially crippling. Does this mean that contentment is anathema to my person? That contentment is a punishing mind-bender (to be content is to be less content than when you weren't content)? That this period of post-college limbo has been encapsulated, in all its dumb, stereotypical hand-wringing, by a bean cake?

Two months later I am spiritually annihilated by contentment.

I haven't had a craving in months, and I'm so worried that I won't desire anything ever again that I forget to worry about my uncertain future. I pack my things, and within twenty-four hours I am on a dawn bus to Phuket, Thailand. Suddenly I am seized by a familiar sense of specific urgency, a hunger disconnected from appetite: I want tekka-don for breakfast. I am on a bus in the south of Thailand, and I want—no, must have—a bowl of Japanese rice and raw tuna. While I'm beside myself with relief, I'm simultaneously aware of the bear hug of my iffy future (no job, no place to live, running out of money) tightening around my chest again with an intensity I interpret as affection. My uncertain future missed me, too. I get off the bus at the beach and stare at the aptly blank horizon. I am broke and aimless, I am racked by doubt and worry, I crave a food that's three thousand miles away and I've never experienced such bliss in my life.

JAPANESE-STYLE WHITE RICE

1. Place 1 3/4 cups Japanese-style short-grain rice in a bowl and cover with cold water. Stir, then drain. Repeat until the water runs clear. Place the rice in a medium-size heavy saucepan and add a scant 2 cups cold bottled water. Let sit for 10 minutes.

2. Place the covered pot over high heat and bring to a rolling boil. Do not lift the lid; the water is boiling when the pot hisses. Reduce heat to medium-low and cook until the water is absorbed, about

5 minutes. Raise heat to high for 30 seconds. Remove from heat and allow rice to stand, covered, for 10 minutes.

Makes 4 cups

TEKKA-DON (MARINATED TUNA OVER RICE)

2 tablespoons soy sauce

1 tablespoon mirin

12 to 14 ounces sashimi-quality fresh tuna

2/3 cup seasoned rice vinegar (sushi su or awase-zu)

2/3 cup rice vinegar (kome-su)

2 tablespoons sugar

1 teaspoon salt

Small piece of kombu (kelp), optional

3 1/2 to 4 cups hot white rice (see recipe)

1/2 sheet toasted nori

Sliced pickled pink ginger (amazu shoga)

1 tablespoon prepared wasabi paste

1. In a shallow glass baking dish, stir together the soy sauce and mirin. Cut the tuna into 1/8-by-1-by-2-inch rectangular slices. Lay the slices in the dish in a single layer, turning them to coat both sides. Cover and refrigerate 2 to 24 hours.

2. In a small saucepan, combine the rice vinegars, sugar, salt and kombu. Heat, stirring, until sugar dissolves. Place the hot rice in

a wide wooden bowl. Cool the rice by tossing it with a spatula while fanning it. When the rice stops steaming, drizzle in about 1 tablespoon of the vinegar mixture. Continue to toss and fan the rice, gradually seasoning with the mixture to taste. Cover with plastic wrap and set aside in a cool, dark place for up to 12 hours; do not refrigerate or freeze.

3. Divide the rice among 4 bowls. Crumble the nori on top. Arrange 6 or 7 slices of tuna over each portion of rice to cover it completely. Top with a ginger rosette and a dab of wasabi paste.

Serves 4

KATSU-DON (PORK CUTLET OVER RICE)

4 lean, boneless pork chops

2 tablespoons all-purpose flour

1 large egg, beaten with 1/2 tablespoon cold water

1 1/2 cups panko (Japanese bread crumbs)

Vegetable oil, for deep frying

2 tablespoons soy sauce

1 tablespoon mirin

1 small yellow onion, thinly sliced

3 jumbo eggs, lightly beaten with 1 tablespoon water

2 to 3 tablespoons cooked peas

2 to 3 cups hot white rice (see recipe)

1/2 sheet toasted nori, crumbled

1 tablespoon pickled red ginger (beni shoga), shredded

1. Score the meat with the tip of a knife, then pound with the side of the knife until 1/4-inch thick. Dust with flour, dip in the egg mixture, and coat with panko.

2. Pour 2 inches of oil in a wok or large skillet and heat to 375 degrees. Fry the chops in batches, turning once, for about 20 minutes, until golden and no longer pink in the center. Let cool, then cut into 1/4-inch strips.

3. In a medium skillet over medium-low heat, combine the soy sauce, mirin and 1/2 cup water. Add the onion and simmer until just wilted. Add the pork strips in 4 clusters. Simmer until pork is warm and there is little liquid in the pan. Pour in the eggs and poach until the edges are set, a little over a minute. Scatter the peas on top. With a spatula, divide the omelet into 4 portions.

4. To serve, divide the rice among 4 bowls and top with an omelet slice and any remaining pan juices. Garnish with nori and ginger.

Serves 4

All recipes adapted from Elizabeth Andoh, the author of *Washoku*.

A Taste of Home

MANIL SURI

Manil Suri, the author of The Death of Vishnu, *is a professor of mathematics at the University of Maryland, Baltimore County. His second novel,* The Age of Shiva, *was published in 2007.*

Growing up in India, I lived with my parents in a single room, part of a flat shared with three other families. Although we were middle class, there were times when our finances dipped to the change I collected in the slotted metal box by my bed. Still, my parents managed to scrimp enough to put me through an elite private school—my ticket to a better future, they said. It was a bittersweet parting when I received a scholarship to study mathematics in America—my parents knew I was leaving behind everything in the life I had shared so closely with them. For the next eight years, I industriously assimilated myself into America. Then, in 1988, a seven-month research sabbatical brought me to Paris.

Now that I had made it to this third continent, a whole new culture awaited exploration. I sat at cafés sipping Pernod and speaking French. I splurged on a nice apartment (Look, Mom and Dad, my own place in Paris!). I started putting mousse in my hair, then styling foam as well. With Europe on my résumé, my promotion from Immigrant to World Citizen seemed within reach.

What truly drew me in was the food. I explored every *marché* I could find, and ate at starred restaurants I could ill afford. I learned to tell the difference between Bordeaux and Burgundy, *Brie* and *Chaource*. Watching the recently released *Babette's Feast* near the end of my stay, I had an idea. Wouldn't it be great to prepare a multicourse French meal for my parents in Bombay to give them a taste of the new world I'd discovered?

Although the steps I'd taken to reinvent myself had, perforce, led me further away from India as well, I still made annual family visits. All year, I would look for recipes (mostly Thai and Chinese) pungent enough to tantalize my relatives' taste buds, taking back jars of ingredients one couldn't get there (*sambal olek* was their favorite). This time, though, I'd expand their horizons further afield, educate their *masala*-conditioned palates on the quieter complexities of *bouillabaisse* and *coq au vin*. It would be as if Dinesen's heroine were making her Asian debut in *Babette Does Bombay*.

By the time I reached India, I had the menu planned. Between the *bouillabaisse* and *coq au vin*, I'd serve something meatless in an herb-accented *sauce béchamel* for my vegetarian aunt. The Camembert I'd picked up at the Charles de Gaulle duty-free would be the appetizer—and I'd prepare a *crème caramel* for dessert. I forbade my mother from making *chappatis* in accompaniment. "You know your father's never satisfied without them," she protested. I replied, "In France, they eat bread."

We couldn't find the Calphalon pot I had given her the year before. "So heavy," my mother said. "Did you think your mother was an American that she could have lifted it?" It was impossible to keep the sugar from scorching in the thin, worn pans she stubbornly clung to, so I decided to replace the *crème caramel* with fruit.

The Grant Road fish market seemed filthier than I remembered—I longed for my pristine neighborhood Marché Raspail. The fisherwomen saw me treading gingerly through the muck in my Nikes and lovingly called me over to sell me their catch at twice the price. The poultry vendor held up a squawking male chicken—a *murgh*—for me, pulling back the feathers to expose its breast. I remembered this ritual from my boyhood—what exactly had my father looked for as he pressed his fingertips like a stethoscope against the flesh? I nodded at the offering without touching it, instantly realizing my mistake from the shopkeeper's sudden jolliness.

My cousin and her husband arrived with my aunt just as I was putting out the Camembert. "It smells even worse than it looks," my mother declared, and refused to touch it. My father, who relished the Laughing Cow processed cheese wedges I occasionally brought as a treat, was more game. Ever since I'd arrived, his knees had been so swollen with arthritis that he couldn't get up—so I cut a piece and brought it to him. He chewed it once, then literally leapt out of bed and went running to the sink to spit it out. The sounds of his furious gargling ensured that none of the other guests dared a taste.

Clearly *fromage* needed travel and training, which my family didn't have—I was sure they'd find my *bouillabaisse* easier to appreciate. I had made the *fumet* with fish trimmings and shrimp shells, using a pinch of saffron and many different types of fish, just as a friend had taught me. To expose my relatives to flavors subtler than they were accustomed to, I had omitted the spicy distraction of the *rouille*. "Note the pure, clean taste of the simply stewed seafood," I instructed as they tasted it.

My cousin spoke first—"Do you still have that chili paste?" I watched in horror as her husband found the jar of *sambal olek* in the refrigerator, then passed it around for people to stir by the spoonful into their soup. More *sambal olek* (and some black beans and green curry paste, too) went into my vegetarian creamed cauliflower and noodle course. "Does it have eggs?" my aunt asked, holding up a strand of pasta as if she could detect flecks of yolk embedded incriminatingly in it. The empty package fished out from the trash said it did, so I ended up making her tomato soup instead, from a packet of Lipton soup mix.

The *coq* fared even worse. The landlord's family, with whom we shared a kitchen, was devout Muslim—wouldn't filling the kitchen with clouds of vaporized wine be regarded as blasphemous? So I decided to make *coq sans vin* instead, adding a glass at the table for flavor. Unfortunately, the *murgh* I'd been sold was so wizened that even its liver proved invulnerable to cooking.

My family milled around the pot, dabbing bits of bread into the wine-soused gravy. "So this is the French curry you think is better than ours?" my cousin remarked. A minor stampede ensued when my mother brought out the rice and chickpeas she'd prepared "just in case." My aunt, still hungry, spotted a dish of leftover *dal* in the refrigerator—it was also scraped clean. I tried to smile—in India, the guest is always right, I repeated to myself.

In the postmortem the next morning, I tried to figure out how I could have created such a culinary disaster. The pasta, at least, had been fine, the *bouillabaisse* correct, so was it really all my cooking to blame? I remembered the years of kitchen implements I had brought back, which my parents refused to use (the chef's knife "huge enough to slaughter a lamb," the vegetable peeler that "ate half the carrot away"). Had my family simply been digging their heels in again, balking at the leap from Indian to rarefied Continental I had pushed them to make? Could my desire to show off my worldliness have been too unvarnished—had they been telling me I had strayed too far, trying to corral me back into the fold again?

I set the uneaten *coq* back on the stove. And dropped in a spoonful of *sambal olek*.

MURGH AU VIN

FOR THE CHICKEN

2 1/2 tablespoons fruity olive oil

2 medium onions, finely chopped

4 large garlic cloves, minced

1 jalapeño, minced

2 teaspoons ground coriander

1 1/2 teaspoons ground cumin

1 cinnamon stick

4 cardamom pods, crushed

6 whole cloves

2 star anise

2 bay leaves

Salt

8 free-range chicken thighs, skins removed

1 bottle (750 ml) dry red wine, like Chianti

TO FINISH

2 scallions, thinly sliced

1 garlic clove, minced

1 inch-long piece ginger, peeled and very thinly sliced

1 cayenne chili, seeded and very thinly sliced (optional)

1/4 cup cilantro leaves

Baguette or cooked basmati rice (optional).

1. Heat the olive oil in a wide, heavy pot over medium heat. Add the onions and sauté until soft and translucent, about 7 minutes. Add the garlic and jalapeño and sauté, stirring until the onion is golden, about 7 minutes more. Add the coriander and cumin and sauté for another 3 minutes or so, then add the cinnamon, cardamom, cloves, star anise, bay leaves and 2 teaspoons salt, and cook, stirring, for about 3 minutes more to release the spice oils.

2. Increase the heat to high, add the chicken and fry on all sides until the meat is no longer pink, about 5 minutes. Add the wine and bring to a boil. Simmer, covered, until the chicken is falling off the bone, about 1 hour. Using a slotted spoon, transfer the chicken pieces to a bowl and keep warm.

3. Increase the heat to high and boil until the liquid has reduced to 2 cups. Remove cinnamon, cardamom, cloves, star anise and bay leaves. Season sauce to taste with salt. Return chicken to the pot and stir until heated through.

4. To finish, add the scallions, garlic, ginger, cayenne (if using) and 3 tablespoons of the cilantro. Stir for 30 seconds, then transfer to a serving bowl and garnish with remaining cilantro. If you choose, serve with baguette or rice.

Serves 4 to 6

Ghosts of Passovers Past

ANNA WINGER

Anna Winger is a photographer and writer living in Berlin. Her first novel, This Must Be the Place, *was published this year.*

Berlin is not the first place most people would choose to celebrate Passover. Although the city now claims a burgeoning Jewish population, there isn't a single kosher butcher, supermarket horseradish is mixed with cream, and as for matzo, well, good luck.

There is no continuum of Jewish life here; no long-standing local traditions remain. The Jews who now live in Berlin are mostly newcomers like me, making things up as we go along. I moved here from New York in 2002, to be with my German husband.

Since then I have held yearly Seders with an increasingly large and diverse group of friends. They are other Jewish New Yorkers and their German partners, a couple of Israelis, a French Jewish family with many daughters, the occasional Latin American Jew and one Norwegian. Last year we were twenty-three in all.

The Passover meal varies from home to home, but there are basic parameters: nothing that contains leavening (bread, beer), no milk at a meal with meat, no pork or shellfish. The elements of the Seder plate (parsley, horseradish, egg, haroset, lamb bone) are always the same. And red wine is important, since each person drinks four times throughout the ceremony and more, if they like, during the meal.

At first the question was not so much what to feed all these guests, as how. You would think it would be easy to pull together a Seder in Berlin, since many typically Jewish foods are mainstream German fare too: potato pancakes with applesauce, poppy-seed cake, rye bread. Sauerbraten looks and tastes a lot like brisket. Even matzo balls bear a striking resemblance to Knödel, starchy balls that are usually served as a side dish with gravy. But the devil is in the details. Knödel, for instance, are made with bread. While many variations are available—whole wheat, spelt, potato flour—unleavened meal of any kind is impossible to come by. (Conversely, when my husband made a traditional German Christmas meal for my family in Cambridge, Mass., last year, duck breasts and red cabbage were easy to find, but when he asked for Knödel mix at

Whole Foods, he was led directly to the wide range of matzo meal in Aisle 4. But that's another story. . . .)

My parents are anthropologists, and as a child, I often lived with them in the remote locations where they tended to do their research. Wherever we were, my mother was ritualistic about American food. We ate fried chicken in the middle of the Masai Mara National Reserve in Africa on the Fourth of July. She drummed up Thanksgiving turkeys in Mexico and Nepal. I was not going to be swayed by the lack of matzo meal in German supermarkets.

And so, in the spirit of potluck, my Seders involve more than a little improvisation. One year, as a symbolic gesture, I ordered a frozen kosher lamb bone for the Seder plate from Munich, but that was overdoing it. We use nonkosher meat from the local organic butcher. The tsimmes is made from sweet potatoes tracked down at a Thai market near our apartment. In the States, chopped liver is made with schmaltz, which poses a problem here: Jewish schmaltz is made from rendered chicken fat, German schmaltz from pork; I use olive oil. One friend makes great horseradish with beets from scratch. Another, who comes from five generations of Jews in Atlanta, makes haroset with grape juice instead of kosher wine. My friend Patricia glazes the roast lamb with Turkish pomegranate syrup. (Berlin has one of the biggest Turkish populations of any city outside of Istanbul, so Turkish products are widely available, and many of them, including freshly baked macaroons, are perfect for Passover.) Handmade chocolate-covered walnuts and an incredible array of dried-fruit delicacies come from the Greek store across the street from me. What appears to be a jewelry store behind KaDeWe, Berlin's largest department store, turns out to be an Israeli food depot selling delicious baba ghanouj and, yes, matzo.

There is a Koscherei in my neighborhood that is rarely open, a small place selling salt, bad wine and good gefilte fish. Just before the holidays, it becomes a crossroads for Jews of every stripe who are united only, perhaps, by the uncanny sensation of preparing for a holiday on what is just a normal working day to the rest of the city. People greet one another in Hebrew or Russian. Sometimes they speak English to me. No one speaks German, although every-body can. We have little in common, but the mood is optimistic because it is an interesting time to be living in Berlin. Sixteen years after reunification, the city is finally coming into its own again. Before the war it was a center of Jewish life, and now we have the opportunity to participate in its rebuilding.

To love Berlin is to accept its history and to live with its ghosts. After we bought our apartment, my husband and I had all the wallpaper stripped and the original walls replastered. In our daughter's room, we found paintings of characters from fairy tales: a blue Puss in Boots, Hansel and Gretel, a grandmother and her gingerbread house. Based on the last layer of wallpaper removed, we were told that these paintings were made around 1930. I went downstairs and asked my oldest neighbor, a man who was born in the building, about the people who lived here then. "A Jewish family," he said. "Almost everyone in our building was Jewish before the war." Then he told me how they had been rounded up in the courtyard and taken away. He didn't remember the event himself, he said, but his mother had described it, and the image had always stayed with him.

I walk through that courtyard every day. In my daughter's room, we plastered around the paintings, leaving them exposed like frescoes, our own makeshift memorial. And when we tell the story of Exodus together around our dining room table each year, we honor the families who lived here before us. We eat tsimmes made with Thai sweet potatoes, roast lamb with Turkish glaze and sweet, Georgian haroset. We celebrate, Jews and Germans together, because Berlin is a city with a terrible past but a promising future, and this is our home now.

BEET HORSERADISH

1 large beet, scrubbed
1/4 pound fresh horseradish (about 4 inches long)
3 tablespoons white balsamic vinegar
1 teaspoon sugar
1 teaspoon salt

Place the beet in a medium pot, cover with water, and bring to a boil. Simmer until the beet is easily pierced with a fork, about 1 hour. Cool, peel, then coarsely grate into a large bowl. Peel the horseradish and grate using a fine grater or food processor. In a small bowl, stir together the horseradish, vinegar, sugar and salt, then pour this over the beets and mix well.

Makes about 2 cups

Adapted from Patricia Ferer.

ROAST LAMB WITH POMEGRANATE GLAZE

FOR THE GLAZE
1 cup pomegranate syrup
1 cup honey
1 cinnamon stick
3 allspice berries
1 garlic clove, crushed
1 sprig rosemary
Juice of 1 lemon

FOR THE LAMB
1 rack of lamb
Olive oil
Salt and freshly ground black pepper

1. Place a roasting pan in the oven and preheat to 450 degrees. To make the glaze: Combine all the ingredients except lemon juice in a small saucepan. Bring to a boil, then simmer for 20 minutes, stirring occasionally. Remove from the heat and strain. Stir in the lemon juice.

2. To make the lamb: Rub the lamb with olive oil and season with salt and pepper. Place in the heated pan, fatty side down, and roast for 10 minutes. Baste with glaze, turn over, and baste the other side. Cook for 10 to 15 minutes, or until a meat thermometer inserted reads 125 degrees. Let stand several minutes before slicing. Serve with extra glaze.

Serves 4

Adapted from Patricia Ferer.

CHOPPED LIVER WITH OLIVE OIL

1/4 cup olive oil

1 large onion, finely chopped

2 large garlic cloves, finely chopped

12 ounces chicken livers, drained

Salt and freshly ground black pepper

4 hard-boiled eggs

Finely chopped flat-leaf parsley (optional)

1. Heat the olive oil in a large sauté pan over medium-high heat. Add the onion and garlic and cook until softened, about 5 minutes. Add the chicken livers and a pinch of salt and sauté, stirring occasionally, until the livers are cooked through, 5 to 7 minutes. Cool the mixture for at least 10 minutes and chop by hand or in a food processor, depending on the consistency you prefer. Season to taste.
2. Mash the eggs, leaving them chunky, and combine with the liver mixture. Add parsley, if using, and more olive oil if desired.

Makes about 2 1/2 cups

POPPY-SEED TORTE

1 1/2 cups poppy seeds
1 teaspoon baking powder or 3 tablespoons potato starch
6 eggs, at room temperature, separated
1 cup sugar
1 teaspoon vanilla extract
7 tablespoons unsalted butter, melted and cooled
Confectioner's sugar

1. Preheat the oven to 300 degrees. Grease a 9-inch springform pan and line the bottom with parchment or waxed paper.
2. Using a coffee grinder, grind the poppy seeds in batches for

about 20 seconds. (The seeds will become slightly sticky.) Combine with the baking powder in a large bowl.

3. In a mixer fitted with a paddle, beat the egg yolks until slightly thickened. Slowly add the sugar and vanilla. Slowly pour in the butter, then add the poppy-seed mixture. Beat until combined. Return the mixture, which will be very thick, to the large bowl.

4. Using a clean bowl and a whisk, beat the egg whites until they form soft peaks. Fold them into the batter and pour it into the prepared pan. Bake for 50 to 60 minutes, or until a toothpick inserted into the center comes out fairly dry. Cool on a wire rack for at least an hour before unmolding. Dust with confectioner's sugar before serving.

Serves 12

Eau God

HENRY ALFORD

Henry Alford has written humor for The *New Yorker, the* New
York Times *and* Vanity Fair. *He is the author of an upcoming
book about the wisdom of old people,* How to Live.

I once cooked away a bad memory.

I'd just been through a difficult breakup with my boyfriend. Over the course of our ten years together, he'd given
me the gift of travel—he'd taken me to Costa Rica once and Italy
six times—and now, to show my fiery, post-divorce mettle, I'd
decided to take myself on a trip someplace exotic and adventure-
some. Someplace he'd never been. I wanted an experience that
would be transporting, and perhaps even sublime.

Morocco.

My guidebook said that, when sightseeing in Morocco, never hire an unofficial guide as they are illegal. But the first thing I did upon stepping outside of my hotel in Marrakesh was to hire an unofficial guide. Mohammed, sporting a djellaba and a huge smile, had a lot going for him—he said he knew the best place to buy spices in the spice market, and he wanted only fifteen dollars for showing me around. This augured well.

We walked to the spice market, a labyrinthine jumble of open-air stalls and dark corners. Suave and twinkly-eyed, Mohammed combined worldly know-how with a lot of dramatic hand gestures—Omar Sharif, for the deaf. I bought cellophane sleeves of turmeric and cumin, thinking of the fabulous tagines I would make when I got home. When a grim-looking vendor had me smell a tiny vial of orange blossom oil, or neroli, I had a spasm of near-synesthesia—I could almost see orange blossoms. Not really knowing what the oil was used for, I bought the vial for about twelve dollars.

Mohammed next took me to the Majorelle Gardens, the luxuriant park just outside Yves St. Laurent's home. He said that I should go in, and that he'd meet me at the entrance at twelve-thirty. But at twelve-thirty, there was no sign of Mohammed. I asked several other guides if they'd seen him, and explained that I hadn't paid him yet; they had not. I waited for half an hour. Mohammed was nowhere to be found.

Back in my hotel room, I grew uneasy. Mohammed knew where I was staying: La Mamounia, the opulent four-star hotel that I'd treated myself to as my Marrakesh entry point. There were several witnesses to the fact that I had not paid him. Would he and the police show up at my door? Then I looked at the spices and the oil. The vendors I'd bought them from were clearly in financial cahoots with Mohammed, as is often the case with guides and vendors. Suddenly my unease metastasized into panic. Oh, my God, I thought, the spices are drugs! Maybe it's Mohammed's m.o. to plant drugs on innocent-looking tourists staying at pricey hotels and then extort money from them! Only in my feverish imagination has the word "turmeric" ever called to mind the word "shakedown." The chain of illogic and anxiety kept ramping and ramping up, threatening to burst from my head like the elevator in *Charlie and the Chocolate Factory.*

I grabbed the spices and the oil, and walked for about five minutes to the most remote part of the hotel, where I found a canister-style ashtray. Biting into the cellophane sleeves to open them, I dumped their contents into the ashy sand and swirled it around: paranoiac Spin Art. Why I thought I needed to empty, rather than simply discard, the sleeves is unclear to me now, but at the time it seemed the only option; it was as if my fear were a free-floating virus and I was its human host. When I opened the vial of orange blossom oil to empty it, too, though, I smelled it again and thought, No, I cannot throw this away. It seemed so pure and goldenny. I couldn't quite put my finger on what it smelled like, and then it struck me. It smelled like the gift soap in heaven. I put it back in my pocket.

I did run into, and pay, Mohammed in front of the hotel the next morning—it turned out he'd been arrested outside the gardens for unofficial guiding—but when I saw him again, he looked about as threatening as a pair of socks. Nevertheless, the anxiety and stress of my spice-jettisoning cast a slight pall over the rest of my trip, barring my entry into the sublime. Ten days after the Spice Incident, having sniffed the oil with a frequency bordering on the abject, I spirited it into my luggage for my flight home. The most redolent thing I'd ever smelled in my life was now synaptically connected to one of the more embarrassing moments in my life.

My research back home revealed that orange flower oil is used primarily in baked goods, but also in fruit salads and in drinks like Ramos Gin Fizzes. I made a lot of madeleines using the *Joy of Cooking*'s recipe and adding ten drops of oil. At first I thought my attraction to this activity was purely gustatory or aesthetic, but I have gradually realized that there is consolation to be found in any baked good that calls for more than one stick of butter. Indeed, the more madeleines I made, the more I associated the fragrant oil with crispy, shell-shaped deliciousness instead of the Spice Incident. In *Remembrance of Things Past,* madeleines are celebrated for their ability to induce memory, but I have used them to erase memory; I am the anti-Proust, and my fountain pen flows with butter. Recently I've gotten into the habit of pouring the batter into a cake pan and slightly undercooking it before glazing the cake with a powdered-sugar-based glaze spiked with orange zest.

I find the cake's—and the madeleines'—taste fairly transporting: just one bite and I'm washing my hands in Heaven.

ORANGE FLOWER MADELEINE CAKE

FOR THE CAKE

3/4 cup unsalted butter, plus more for greasing pan

1 cup cake flour, sifted, plus more for dusting pan

2 large eggs

1 cup sugar

1 teaspoon vanilla

1/8 teaspoon dilution of 10% neroli (orange flower) oil (see Note)

FOR THE GLAZE

1/2 cup confectioner's sugar, sifted

1 tablespoon plus 2 teaspoons whole milk, hot

1/2 teaspoon vanilla

2 teaspoons finely grated orange zest

1. Preheat the oven to 350 degrees. Butter an 8-inch cake pan. Place a round of parchment on the bottom, butter the parchment, and dust the entire pan with flour, tapping out the excess.
2. In a small saucepan, melt the butter. Cool to lukewarm and skim the white solids off the top.
3. In the bottom of a double boiler bring 1 inch of water to a

very low simmer. Set the top over it, add the eggs and whisk until lukewarm. Whisk in the sugar. Remove from heat and beat until thick, pale and creamy, incorporating as much air as possible. When cool, gradually fold in the cake flour. Mix in the melted butter, vanilla and neroli oil. Transfer to the cake pan and bake until a toothpick inserted in the middle comes out nearly clean and the cake is golden, 22 to 25 minutes. Cool completely on a wire rack. Using a knife, separate the edge of the cake from the pan. Turn the cake out onto a plate.

4. Prepare the glaze: Put the confectioner's sugar into a bowl. Stir in the milk, vanilla and orange zest. Spread over the top of the cake.

Serves 12

Adapted from *Joy of Cooking.*

Note: A dilution of 10% neroli (orange flower) oil with 90% flavorless sweet almond oil is available at Aphrodisia Herbe Shoppe, 264 Bleeker Street, (212) 989-6440. A 1/3-ounce bottle is $18.00. Half a teaspoon of orange flower water may be substituted for the orange flower oil, but it will lack the intensity and flavor of the oil.

Family Menu

ALLEN SHAWN

*Composer and writer Allen Shawn teaches at Bennington Col-
lege. He is the author of* Wish I Could Be There.

F or my sister, who has lived in an institution in Maryland
for the mentally retarded since she was eight years old,
there's no hiding the fact that food is central. When she
is eating, it appears to be very much the focus of her attention,
and she doesn't like to be distracted from it by conversations, let
alone by dramatic events. In anticipating the birthday lunches my
parents planned for her on her yearly trips to their summer rental
in Bronxville, New York—trips to which she would be brought
by a member of the staff of the place where she lives, and which

would last no more than two hours—she would always reel off the menu she was expecting. This meal never varied throughout her teenage years and remained unchanged as she passed through her twenties, thirties, forties and fifties: chicken salad, tomatoes, rolls with butter, iced tea, ice cream and cake. Each summer when she would come to the Bronxville house, she would be sure to mention the food again within a few moments of arriving. Mary has a way of speaking that can almost be like singing or intoning, with each syllable being given enormous weight. This menu list always sounded particularly emphatic. During the chicken salad course, she would mention a few times that ice cream and cake were coming later.

My sister Mary is fifty-nine years old. So am I. We are twins. These days, children with the combination of autism, mental retardation and elements of schizophrenia from which she suffers are rarely institutionalized, and are more likely to live in a kind of group home. Indeed, even the notion of "suffering" I just suggested has come to look a bit suspect, since it implies that it is "best" for a person not to have certain "deficits." And I am no longer certain that she suffers more than others, only that her distress can be more immediately obvious than the distress of others when it hits her, and harder to comprehend. Mary has a personality, and experiences and an inner life that can't be easily evaluated either by testing her, or even by hearing what she has to say, since limited verbal communication is at the heart of what ails her. I spent my early childhood trying to read her. So did my parents.

My parents always maintained that it would upset Mary to return to the apartment in New York where she spent her first eight years, even if only for a two-hour lunch. Therefore even when my older brother and I had reached advanced middle age, our father had died, and our mother's health and mental sharpness had declined to such an extent that she couldn't go to Bronxville anymore, we held the yearly lunches in a private hotel dining room, rather than in the familiar apartment where our mother still lived, and had the hotel prepare the exact menu we had always made for Mary in Bronxville.

By summer 2005, it was clear that our mother would not last much longer. She was ninety-nine years old, unable to move her hands or legs, or to take care of herself in any way. She had also not even spoken for many months, was profoundly hard of hearing, and would only open her eyes for a few minutes at a time.

Our friends Amy and Piergiorgio were now living with her, and, along with an extraordinary woman named Marjorie, helping to take care of her. Piergiorgio prepared wonderful soft dishes for her which she was fed, with her eyes remaining, for the most part, closed. In those last weeks, even when Amy would read to her, our mother, who had been a journalist and brilliantly verbal person her entire life, no longer gazed raptly up at her face, as she used to do, but remained curled up in her sleep, in her darkness.

Together—Amy, Piergiorgio, Marjorie, my brother and his girlfriend and I—decided to organize a birthday lunch for Mary in the apartment. We were worried about whether Mary would be shocked to see her mother in such a debilitated state in her wheelchair—unable perhaps to recognize her, to talk with her or hug her, and possibly remaining asleep the entire time—and we were equally concerned that Mary might suddenly explode in some kind of blind fury at the sight of the apartment which she hadn't seen since the age of eight. I racked my brains for the precise lunch items we needed—the exact type of rolls, for example. Amy reminded our mother about the upcoming lunch every day, whispering directly into her ear. I purchased a birthday cake and ice cream; my brother bought presents; Marjorie brought balloons. At the last moment, in addition to the chicken salad and tomatoes and rolls prepared by Amy, Piergiorgio decided to produce an antipasto plate brimming with salami, prosciutto, mozzarella, Brie, olives, and tomatoes with basil, while Marjorie prepared a huge watermelon with sliced fruits inside, and an elaborate salad. These dishes looked as startling to me in this context as a pork loin at a Seder—but it was too late to worry.

Escorted by an aide, Mary arrived dressed in a snappy striped shirt and pink summer pants. She had a particularly comfortable, confident air. In fact, it was as if she knew her way around. Although she asked where the bathroom was, she walked to it as if from long-buried habit. Her comfort in the apartment, and with our mother, was self-evident. But this was the least of the surprises. At the lunch table she ate her helpings of chicken salad and rolls and tomatoes, to be sure, but she was particularly taken with the antipasto, which she asked for second and third helpings of, while asking for more of all of everything by name. She dug into the watermelon and fruit and the unexpected salad with obvious delight and interest. More than once she said that she was having a wonderful time.

And all of this occurred in the presence of a miracle. From the moment our mother was brought into the room, her eyes remained open in unmistakable amazement, wonder and joy, as she looked from one of us to the other in astonishment and gratitude, galvanized, awakened, transfixed, radiantly fulfilled by the sight of her daughter. The occasion roused her and brought her back from a kind of somnolence that had lasted for months, as if encountering bright daylight after an age of darkness. Her eyes remained opened even after Mary had left, and that night she barely slept.

It is amazing how much people contain that we do not ever have a chance to know about, how vast and mysterious we all are. I thought back to this birthday lunch when, only a few months later, we were remembering our mother. And how could I not cry when Piergiorgio recited these lines in Italian from a poem by Salvatore Quasimodo:

Ognuno sta solo sul cuor della terra
Trafitto da un raggio di sole:
Ed è subito sera.

(Everyone stands alone on the heart of the earth
Transfixed by a sun-ray:
And suddenly it is evening.)

Crossing to Safety

DOROTHY ALLISON

Dorothy Allison is the author of Bastard Out of Carolina *and* Cavedweller. *She is working on a new novel,* She Who.

G ravy is the simplest, tastiest, most memory-laden dish I know how to make: a little flour, salt and pepper, crispy bits of whatever meat anchored the meal, a couple of cups of water or milk and slow stirring to break up lumps. That's it. It smells of home, the door locked against the night and a stillness made safe by the sound of a spoon going round in a pan. It is anticipation, the last thing prepared before the meal comes to the table, the bowl in Mama's hand closing the day out peacefully, no matter what came before.

My mother's gravy was a savory country gravy, heavy on the black pepper. Best of all was steak—cube steak. People call it country-fried steak, but Mama always called it cube steak. She began with odd, indented slabs of cheap meat carried home from the diner where she was on her feet all day. My sisters and I would pound the "steak" while she rested. The little round mouth of the Coke bottle thudded into the meat over and over until each piece was not only dimpled but flattened out half again as wide as it had been. By the time Mama stopped us, the steaks would be tenderized almost to pieces. Then she would shoo us out of the way, make up the biscuits and sift some of the flour onto a plate. Dredged in flour, the steaks went into a hot cast-iron skillet with a good covering of bacon fat. So long as we set the table and were useful, we were allowed to watch Mama cook the steaks and then set them aside on a brown paper bag. Then she took the plate of leftover flour and sprinkled it in the pan, stirring it as it browned and the pan filled with little brown flour pebbles and charred bits of meat. A lot of water and a little milk made steam rise up in a sweet cloud. Mama worked the gravy with a fork until all was smooth and silky. She might pour the gravy over the steaks or she might serve it in a bowl. It was not until I was grown that I understood that gravy poured over the meat before it came to the table meant there was not much meat.

In one tract house or another, first in South Carolina and then Florida, where we moved when I was a teenager, Mama made magic with cheap meat, flour and determination—hiding from us how desperate things might be. She did such a good job of it that we came to believe cube steak a luxury, better than the rare T-bone our uncles might bring around as a surprise.

My son, Wolf, was born when I was past forty and the author of a best-selling novel. That means he has grown up a middle-class child—one who sometimes asks me for stories of my childhood but knows nothing of what it means to grow up poor and afraid. I have worked to make sure of that. His favorite foods are all dishes I never even knew existed until I was a voting adult: spinach soufflés, steamed mussels and sautéed brussels sprouts. He has almost never eaten an egg yolk and never took an interest in gravy, not even on Thanksgiving turkey.

"No thank you," he said, very politely.

My feelings were hurt. How could my child not like my gravy? Maybe it was the giblets I chopped and added? Next time I made a smooth, pristine gravy with no bits of anything. Wolf didn't touch it.

This time I sighed. I had to face the truth. My gravy was nowhere near as good as my mother's had been, and my son was not me. He had never gone to bed hungry and had no idea how important a locked door could be. I could not be unhappy about that.

Then there was the duck.

It was three years ago, and I wanted to do something special for the holidays to celebrate our aunt Mary moving up from Arizona. At the grocery, there was a big sale sign—ducks and geese at discount. A duck, a goose, a British Christmas dinner. I had read the novels. I had a brand-new roasting pan. So just because I could, I bought one of each—the goose for Christmas and the duck for New Year's.

Christmas was wonderful, but the goose was not a success. It came out pretty but dry. I stripped the leftovers for the dogs and worried. What was I going to do with that duck? I thought about giving up and making a ham. But my pride got in my way. I could cook. I was my mother's daughter.

It was clear to me that what was going to be necessary was a gravy—a good gravy. I read up on ducks and followed directions. I hung the bird over the sink in the warm kitchen and watched the fat drip off. After a while the bird looked greasy but lean. I shooed everyone out and went back to basics. There was no bacon fat in my fridge, but there was bacon. I wrapped the duck in bacon, threw an obscuring layer of aluminum foil over the top and put it in the roasting pan.

You could smell the bacon in the steam coming out the top of the oven, but maybe I was the only one who noticed. It was New Year's after all, with family and friends and lots of dishes. There were greens and black-eyed peas and sweet potatoes with marshmallows. There were pies and loud music—lots of things to distract everyone away from the oven.

When the duck was done, I set it on a platter and disappeared the bacon slices. Then I poured off almost all the grease and took a spoon after the blackened bits in the bottom of the pan. Maybe the duck would be dry as the goose had been. But the bits in the bottom of the pan looked like great cracklings. I scraped and dredged and turned on the heat, then sprinkled flour and pepper across the oily surface. It cooked into the familiar brown pebbles. I squeezed a bite between my fingers and tasted salty, rich flavor. Uh-huh. A cup of skim milk brought up steam through which I stirred steadily. Another cup went after the first, then a cup of water. I used a fork to squash the lumps and kept stirring. Every now and then I would taste the gravy again and then go searching in my cupboard. Yes, more black pepper and a little bottled magic from K-Paul's Louisiana Kitchen. At the last minute I reached over and spooned in some of the creamy liquid off the black-eyed peas. It made me laugh—but the gravy smelled wonderful.

Soon there were offers to help carry in the dishes. My son was standing by me at the stove. He was staring at the gravy I was still stirring. He leaned forward over the pan.

"Mmm."

I looked at him. His big green eyes were wide and hungry. I used a wooden spoon. Blew on the gravy to cool it, then let him lick a taste.

"Oh, that's wonderful!" he said.

After that everyone was quick to the table. The duck was per-fect, everyone said so. I felt as if I had passed some ancient rite or earned some essential vindication. There was no gravy left when the meal was done.

Every now and then, I make duck again. But more often, I do what I know. I roast a chicken or pan-fry a steak and make pan gravy to go with it. Sometimes my boy comes to watch me cook. I watch him. He is getting so tall, now four inches taller than I and growing fast, while the world looms ever larger and more uncertain. I try not to worry. I try to make him feel he is home and safe and will always be so, no matter what comes to the door.

ROAST DUCK

1 4-to-6-pound duck
1/2 cup peeled and halved baby onions
1/2 cup chopped carrots
2 tablespoons butter, cut into cubes
1/2 teaspoon dried savory, sage or thyme
Salt and freshly ground pepper
6 thick slices bacon
1/4 cup flour
3/4 cup whole milk

1. Preheat the oven to 350 degrees. Remove the duck giblets. If you choose, chop and sauté the giblets and set them aside to toss into the gravy later.

2. Prick the duck's skin with a fork. Rinse and pat dry with paper towels. Twist the wing tips under the back and place the duck, breast side up, on a rack set in a roasting pan. Stuff onions, carrots and butter into the cavity. Sprinkle the duck all over with the dried herbs and 1/2 teaspoon each of salt and pepper. Lay bacon slices crosswise over the breast. Roast duck in the oven until the internal temperature reaches 170 degrees, 1 1/2 to 2 hours.

3. Place duck on a serving platter and tent with foil. Remove vegetables from cavity. (Check to see if the vegetables are edible. If still raw, microwave until tender and feed to the dogs.)

4. Prepare the gravy by pouring off all but 3 tablespoons of the fat from the pan. Place the pan over medium heat. Using a wooden spoon, scrape up the burned bits stuck to the bottom and then sprinkle with the flour. Cook, stirring, to toast the flour, about 3 minutes. Add the milk and 1/2 cup water. Bring to a boil, then reduce the heat and simmer. If too thick, loosen with water. Season with salt and pepper to taste.

Serves 4 to 6

ACKNOWLEDGMENTS

Putting together a column in the *New York Times Magazine* requires the imaginative collaboration of many people. I'd like to thank my wonderful colleagues Kathy Ryan, Kira Pollack, Joanna Milter, Clinton Cargill, Luise Stauss, Stacey Baker and Masood Kamady in the photo department; Janet Froelich, Rem Duplessis, Cathy Gilmore-Barnes and Nancy Harris in the art department; and all the skillful copy and layout editors at the magazine. And, of course, my bosses who supported the column and this book in the first place: Bill Keller, Gerry Marzorati and Stefano Tonchi.

In particular, I am grateful to Christine Muhlke and Alix Browne, who each edited a number of the columns while I was on leave, and especially to Jill Santopietro, who, in addition to doing editing work, developed many of the recipes included here, and tested and spruced up those that came from other sources.

I'd also like to thank Alex Ward, Tomi Musata, Lee Riffaterre, Merrill Stubbs (who created the frangipane pear tart recipe), Jacqueline Barba, my editor Jill Bialosky, Jeannie Luciano, my agent Heather Schroder and my husband Tad Friend.

Lastly, I am indebted to our writers for their vivid contributions to the canon of meals eaten and remembered.